JUST DAD

STORIES OF HERMAN HOEKSEMA

JUST DAD

LOIS E. KREGEL

REFORMED
FREE PUBLISHING
ASSOCIATION
Jenison, Michigan

Scripture cited is taken from the King James (Authorized) Version

Cover design by Ivan Terzic/www.nadavisual.com
Interior design by Katherine Lloyd/www.the DESKonline.com

Reformed Free Publishing Association
1894 Georgetown Center Drive
Jenison, Michigan 49428
616-457-5970
www.rfpa.org

ISBN 978-1-936054-54-1
Ebook ISBN 978-1-936054-55-8

LCCN 2014952959

In memory of my beloved husband, Chuck,
who went to glory in March, 2014

CONTENTS

PREFACE

It was never my intention to write the story of my father's life. My sister-in-law, Gertrude Hoeksema, had already done that as the author of *Therefore Have I Spoken*. She came to me shortly after Dad died in September of 1965 and said, "Someone ought to write a biography of Dad, and I think I should be the one to do it." I simply said, "Go ahead if you want to." And she did.

Not long ago that book went out of print. The Reformed Free Publishing Association approached me regarding possible changes, since they did not want to reprint the book as it was. I did not simply want to add to it or revise it, if that were even ethical. Yet I had always been aware that Trude was in her twenties before she married my brother Homer, and that she could not have experienced life with our family in the parsonage.

So I decided to tell Dad's story myself, and this is the finished product: a book of tales for the telling and for remembering Dad with love.

Chapter 1

❧

GRONINGEN

Herman Hoeksema was many things: preacher, teacher, student, scholar, blacksmith, carpenter, artist; but to me, he was just Dad.

I did not hear about his early life as a continuous story simply related to me like a novel. It was not like that at all. Rather, the family often gravitated to the living room for a while after the dishes were done, unless Dad had a meeting to lead or a catechism class to teach. If he was spending the evening at home, we might ask him to tell us a story.

We liked his stories; some of them went back to his childhood, some to his youth and adolescence, but all told of a life of which we knew nothing, a life of the streets. It makes you wonder at the ways of God. Why would God choose this waif, toughened and schooled in the ways of the street, to be his faithful servant for so many years? It reminds me of a favorite theme of Dad's, one he often voiced in his sermons: God sometimes chooses the most unlikely persons to be his servants, so that he may receive the glory. This book is an attempt to make a continuous story out of the bits and pieces he told us about his life.

My earliest memory of him is of the day his beloved mother died. I was around three years old. My mother set me on that old mohair davenport in the living room and said, "You must be very quiet today around Papa because his mother died, and he will be very sad."

I have only a faint memory of his mother. We called her "Chicago Grandma" because she lived in Chicago and our other grandma, my mother's mother, lived in Grand Rapids. We had a picture of Chicago Grandma that showed a rather slim woman, dressed in black, sitting in a straight chair with an open Bible in her lap.

I was my father's youngest daughter. The parsonage at 1139 Franklin Street in Grand Rapids, Michigan, is the only home I remember until I was married. It was a big house: upstairs were four bedrooms, a hall that ran the length of the house from front to back, one and a half baths, and a door that opened onto a tin deck, used at various times for sunning, for airing clothes, or for housing pigeons. At the front of the hall was my father's study. There was another door next to it that led to the attic; we might not play there because there was no railing around the stairwell.

Downstairs was a living room, dining room, sun room, office (and reception room for callers),

Dad's mother, Johanna Bakkema
(Chicago Grandma)

breakfast room, kitchen, pantry, hallway, half bath, and play-room-sewing room. Between the kitchen and breakfast room was a swinging door. Behind that door was a button. The button was connected to a buzzer that rang in Dad's study. My mother used that buzzer to summon my father if he had a caller, that is, if he had a caller whom Mom deemed worthy to invite in. She did not lightly invite a caller to come in. If she had, Dad would have gotten little of his work done. If the buzzer in the study rang, Dad would come downstairs. Mom did not often make a mistake.

We called the room to the left of the front doorway and hall the office. Dad received most of his callers there. It also housed our piano, and sometimes we studied in that room or learned our assigned scripture verses on Sunday afternoons, a ritual reserved only for my brother Homer and me. (When my sisters were little, they learned the Heidelberg Catechism; I do not know what my brother Herm learned. Today I thank my dad for it.) That was the house where I grew up.

Often after dinner the family would gather for a while in the living room. Usually it was one of my brothers who would beg Dad for a story. If Dad had to leave in a few minutes to go next door to church for a meeting, or to teach a catechism class, he would have to refuse. But sometimes he would begin, "There was a farmer who had a little pig, and that pig had a curly tail, and oh! That farmer was mad." We would say, "Not that one; that isn't a story. Tell us a real one. Tell us about the time the farmer held you under his pump." We knew most of his stories, but we enjoyed hearing them again.

My father and his cronies had been urchins on the streets of Groningen in the Netherlands. How did this happen?

Dad's mother, Johanna Bakema, had married Tiele Hoek-sema, a handsome cobbler. How this had come to be, I do not

Tiele Hoeksema, Dad's father

know. Whether Johanna's parents disapproved, I do not know. Dad never spoke of any relatives or grandparents except for his Uncle Lulof, his mother's brother. I wish we had asked him.

Johanna and Tiele moved out of Groningen to a suburb called Hoogezand. There Everdiene, their only daughter, was born. Three sons followed: Harm (my father), Albert, and John. Even before Harm was born, Tiele had taken to drinking and philandering. When my father was born on March 12, 1886, Tiele was too drunk to register the birth, and it was March 13 before he went to the clerk's office. Thereafter Dad celebrated his birthday on March 13, but he often said, a little ruefully, that it should have been celebrated on March 12. Finally Tiele abandoned his family altogether and joined the military service of the Netherlands. It would be many years before they heard from him.

Johanna was in desperate straits, but she was strong and resourceful. She moved her family back to the more densely populated city of Groningen, found lodging that opened on the street, and let it be known that she was a good seamstress. Soon she found as many customers as she could satisfy. It was a meager income and out of it she first set aside money for the church they attended and for the Christian school, thereby setting an example for all of her children and grandchildren.

Their home was one room. They had a bed in the wall, and the whole family slept in it. In order to fit they had to lie in opposite directions, so that one's feet were in the other's face—"his

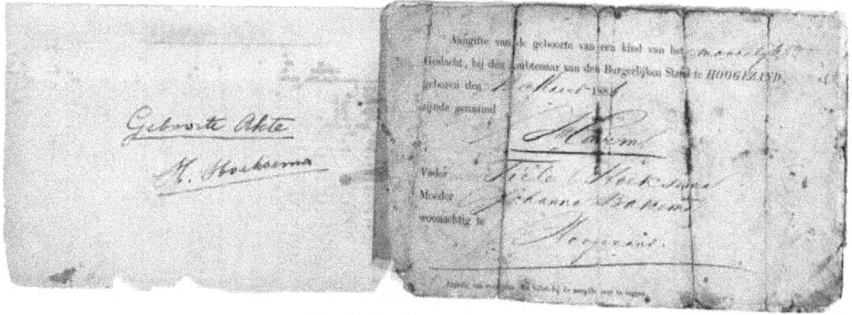

Dad's birth certificate

Dad's boyhood home

dirty feet," as Dad once said from the pulpit, to the chagrin of my mother.

Because she worked as a seamstress in the homes of wealthy clients, Johanna had to be away from her children all day, with only the neighbors trying to keep an eye on them. Everdiene, the oldest, was only a child herself. Who can even begin to imagine that situation? There were no toys or books, nothing but a bare room. Their chairs and table were cardboard boxes.

In those days there was much class distinction. The poor were despised, even in the church, to its shame. The church did not help them at all but looked down on them.

Periodically the bread wagon would come around. Harm and his siblings hated to go there and did so only when they were famished. They had to stand and wait for the piece of dark bread that was thrown to them and then submit to a humiliating search of their pockets to make sure they took no bread home with them. That was how the government helped its poor.

At home in that bare room Harm tried to amuse his younger brothers. He would take a crumb, tie it to a piece of string, and lure one of the many mice out of its hole in the wall. Then he would pull the string around the room just out of the animal's reach, while his brothers looked on in delight.

When that got tiresome, he took to the streets. At five years old he was an urchin on the streets of Groningen. It was not long before Harm found friends who were also looking for fun—and sometimes food. That was how it came to be that Harm and his cronies were stealing apples from a farmer on their way home from school. Usually they posted a lookout, but the lookout was slow to give warning, and the farmer discovered them. All of the boys got away except Harm, who was short and stocky, and slow of foot. The farmer caught him and doused him under the water pump. Harm went home soaking wet and without any apples. This was one of our favorite stories.

On Sundays Johanna took the children to church and also taught them catechism, scripture, psalms, and whatever was good for them. She was strict about Sabbath observance, almost legalistic. One Saturday night, after she had been working all day, she remembered that she had not sewn the white collar on her only black dress. She quickly wielded her needle and her task was finished. Then she glanced at the clock and realized that it was past midnight and already Sunday. Just as quickly she took out the stitches, and on Sunday she wore the dress without the white collar. Dad himself never was quite so legalistic about the Lord's day, but he respected his mother for her piety, for he himself told us this story about her.

Harm and his buddies did much of their mischief when they were on their way home from school. Sometimes the boys would stop at the back of the syrup factory, where there were barrels of syrup stored. While a lookout was posted, they would pry off the cover of a barrel of syrup, dip a fist into the sticky stuff, and run, licking off the syrup as they ran.

All of the boys smoked clay pipes. For tobacco they used cigar butts picked off the streets. Sometimes they would fill their clay pipes with water, and then one of them would approach a gentleman who was smoking a cigar and ask, "A light, *Mijnheer?*" When the gentleman obliged, he would douse the man's cigar, and the boys would run away laughing.

Sometimes Harm would offer to entertain some of those same gentlemen with some poem or a section from scripture. The gentleman understood, of course, that he would have to reward the lad. Then Harm would take his coins and buy a little candy or tobacco.

Many of his exploits involved food; the reason for that is not hard to see. He was hungry, always hungry. Sometimes the boys could not resist the smell of the fresh-baked bread on the back of the bakery wagon, and they would steal a loaf or two and run, eating as they ran. This was one of the stories my mother did not like him to tell us. She might say as we were gathered in the living room, "Not that one, Harm." (She still sometimes called him Harm, his Dutch name, which he changed to Herman when he emigrated to the United States.) My mother probably thought we might get the idea that stealing was sometimes permissible, but that was not the case.

The story did, however, evoke sympathy for those who were so hungry that they would even steal to satisfy their hunger. As for Dad, his feelings showed in his preaching. He sometimes admonished the employers in the congregation to pay their employees a just wage, even when he had to warn the workers against membership in the ungodly labor unions. This was especially true during the Great Depression.

As Harm and his buddies became older, around eleven or so, their exploits became bolder. We enjoyed hearing about those adventures too. We might say, "Tell us about the time you got caught swimming in the canal."

Harm and his pals had been swimming in one of the canals, an activity that was forbidden by law. A policeman saw him swimming, holding his clothing above his head, and called to him to come back to shore. Instead, Harm swam to the other side, donned his clothes, thumbed his nose at the policeman, and ran. My mother did not like that story. It is easy to see why. It was probably one of our favorites, perhaps because Dad was such a firm disciplinarian, and we took some comfort in the fact that he once could have used a firm hand himself.

It was about this time in his life that his father suddenly appeared on the scene. One day as Harm was on his way home from school, he felt a firm hand on his collar and looked up to see the face of his father. He must have sensed it was his father because Harm could scarcely have recognized him after he had not seen him for so many years. His father intended to take him to the place where he was living. Harm struggled with him in an effort to get away, but to no avail.

Then he tried a ruse. He told his father that he had to use

the street urinal, and when his father relinquished his grasp, he ran. As usual, he was slow, and his father quickly recaptured him and took him to his lodgings. Harm began screaming and yelling, and he made such a commotion that his dad was glad to release him and send him on his way. Thereafter his Uncle Lulof, his mother's brother, helped Johanna get separate maintenance (what we would call a restraining order or a personal protection order—something very unusual in those days), so that never again was Harm bothered by his dad.

I remember asking Dad if he thought his father really had a soft spot for him, and he just said, as he looked away, "I don't know." But I always thought that deep down he wished for a real dad.

In the winter the boys went skating on the canals. The winters were not as cold as ours in Michigan, and the ice was never very thick. Harm still tended to be rather clumsy and sometimes fell through; yet he always came back for more. Skating was always a favorite sport of his. Even later on if nearby Reeds Lake in Grand Rapids was frozen over, he would find time to do a little skating.

When Harm was finished with grade school, his mother faced the question of where he should go next. He had done well in school, but he was not the top scholar. Again they consulted with Uncle Lulof, Johanna's brother, who suggested that Harm should try for a scholarship at Ambacht School. There were two students equally worthy of a scholarship. Harm was one of them. Harm's mother was to choose the piece of paper with the name of the winner on it. She reached for the slip farthest from her, then changed her mind, and her good manners took over: "No, I was taught to take the closest," she said. That was the winner.

Harm was to go to Ambacht School. Harm's mother said quietly, "That was the hand of God."

Ambacht School was a school where one could learn a trade, but it was more. A student could also pursue an avocation, something that would enrich his life for years to come. Harm learned to paint with oils there, even though he pursued the trade of blacksmithing. Uncle Lulof was a blacksmith and that influenced Harm, no doubt. Those days at Ambacht School were happy ones for him, and he often talked about them. His life on the streets was over, but his propensity for mischief was not.

He liked and respected his teachers—except for one: the students called him *"De peukel"* (the pimple), for obvious reasons. He was dull and crabby and not likable. The boys were not charitable to him either.

One morning, after the boys had snowballed him after he came to school and he was in a foul mood, he decided to take it out on a student who had misbehaved. After calling the boy to the front of the room, he asked him, *"Sta je goed?"* ("Are you ready?") And then in front of the whole class he gave the boy a kick that sent him flying across the room. He lay there for a few moments, while the class sat stunned and disbelieving. In the silence that followed, Harm said in a clear voice, *"Wat gemeen!"* ("How mean!") For that the teacher promptly sent him to the principal's office. Soon he returned and took his seat, saying nothing. When the teacher could no longer contain himself, he said to Harm, "Well, did you tell the principal?" Harm replied, "Yes." Then the teacher said, "What did he say?" "He said, 'Tell your teacher that I have no time for such trifles.'" When Dad told us this story, you could tell that he was reliving the story and enjoying it in the telling.

Those days at Ambacht School passed swiftly for Harm. At graduation he received a silver watch. He was fifteen and had learned many skills that would later prove useful and enriching, but for now he had to have a job.

He was apprenticed to a country blacksmith for thirty dollars a year plus room and board. It was another experience that increased his sympathy for the laboring man. Each day he was awakened at four o'clock, and he could not go to bed until ten o'clock at night. He spent each day sharpening plowshares and shoeing horses. He had to make both the shoes and the nails. The work was exhausting and the hours were long, but he rather enjoyed it in spite of the scars he received from the work. (He could identify these scars for us when we asked him.)

Dad (Harm) at sixteen

What he did not enjoy was the niggardliness and hypocrisy of the country blacksmith. Again Harm was hungry. The portions of food were small, and if Harm asked for a little more, he was refused. Even worse than that, when the man was about to ask a blessing, he held his cap over his face and said, "Let's peek in the cap a moment," and proceeded to mumble a few meaningless words. Harm was repelled.

After his year of apprenticeship was finished, Harm left that job and went to work for a blacksmith in Groningen who made ornamental fences. Harm took pride in that work, and many years later when he returned for a visit, he could still identify some of the fences he had made. He could once more live with his family too, although he never told us where they were living and if their situation had improved. We never thought to ask him, perhaps because we were so young when he told us these stories. His own financial situation was better: he was earning more money as an iron worker and even saving some.

Harm's older sister, Everdiene, had emigrated to the United States; from there she wrote glowing accounts of life in America, and more and more Harm's thoughts turned there too. The economic situation in the Netherlands had not improved. The situation in the church that Harm attended was also unsatisfactory. The two groups that had resulted from two different reformations in the nineteenth century, the *Afscheiding* and the *Doleantie*, had merged, but only on paper. There were still two groups, each with its own congregations. Harm was partial to the B group and sometimes went to a B church with his friend. His mother belonged to an A church. Harm admired Dr. Abraham Kuyper, who was a leader in the B church.

Harm did not appreciate this division in the churches. Perhaps God was beginning to move him to go into the ministry; I rather think so. At any rate, he made the decision to emigrate. He must have planned to send for his mother and two younger brothers too, even as he bade them goodbye.

Chapter 2

∾

AMERICA

It was with some trepidation that Harm boarded the *Rotterdam*, the ship that was to take him to the United States of America. He was eighteen and alone, and not conversant in English, the language of the country to which he was going. He had said good-bye to his mother and brothers, hoping to see them soon.

He did find others aboard that ship—others from his native land with whom he could have some conversation. It was a time of much emigration. The year was 1904. Nonetheless, when he landed in this new country amid the sights and sounds of busy New York City, when he had been processed through Ellis Island on the eleventh day of May, he was more than a little bewildered. He had had a smooth voyage and had enjoyed the ocean. He had not been the least bit seasick. Now he was hungry and had very little money left, not even enough to buy a little lunch.

He found the train he was to take to Chicago, where Everdiene lived. The price was included in his ship ticket. As he was getting settled in his seat with his meager luggage, he spotted a vendor with pastries coming toward him up the aisle. When he came closer, Harm saw a particularly tempting item and pointed to it, showing his few coins. The vendor indicated that it was enough,

Early Chicago days

and so Harm relished his first piece of apple pie. Immediately it became his favorite. Sometimes, when many years later he was enjoying apple pie at the home of one of his children, he would tell us this story again.

He came to his sister Everdiene's house on the west side of Chicago. Later that area was called Ashland; I do not know when it acquired this name. We knew his sister as Aunt Dena and her husband as Uncle Cos. Aunt Dena was a strong personality; Uncle Cos was not.

Almost immediately Harm went looking for work. He never told us how he traveled, but as he was penniless, he must have walked. He was eager to save enough to send for his mother and two younger brothers. He tried not to think about them too much.

The first job he found was at a blacksmith shop not far away. That looked promising for obvious reasons, but he was probably a little naïve. He had worked only a few days before his fellow workers invited him to go to a meeting. He had no idea of the nature of that meeting and was just beginning to understand the English language a little better, so he went along with them.

He had been sitting down only a few minutes when the chairman asked him to stand and raise his right hand. Then he asked him a question. Harm surmised that he was being asked to swear an oath, and he said no. The chairman asked him again, and again he said no. Upon that, he left the meeting. At the door he was shown the secret handshake for the next meeting. Harm realized he had been working at a union shop, and of course he would not join a union. I say "of course," but I do not know whether he had been taught already in the Netherlands that membership in an ungodly union was not compatible with a godly walk. That was the end of his first job.

He held a one-day job as a delivery man. He did not know that the workers were on strike until at the end of the day, when he was returning the team of horses and the delivery wagon, he was beaten up by a couple of teamsters. He did not know that he was being used as a strike breaker. He quit that job too.

He was willing to try almost anything. He even shoveled cinders out of basements. It was not worth the back-breaking effort.

Then he found a job he liked with the Aermotor Windmill Company. He worked there as a blacksmith. This company made ornamental iron work, such as he had enjoyed making in the Netherlands.

Almost immediately he was told to assemble some steel towers. Harm could see right away that the sections would not fit, and he told the foreman. The foreman told him to put them together anyway, but when Harm tried to do that they toppled over. The foreman was desperate; he had a deadline to meet.

Harm offered to start over, even making new blueprints, a skill he had learned in Ambacht School. His employer was surprised when he volunteered to do that, but he had no other option. Harm finished the job, met the deadline, and earned the admiration of his employer, who assured him that his fortune was made. But that employer was surprised and disappointed when Harm informed him that he was going to study for the ministry.

I don't know just when Harm made that decision. Certain it is that he had been well instructed by his godly mother. It is equally certain that he did not appreciate the confusion in the churches in the Netherlands, with the A churches and B churches, but you would think that he would have been repelled and not encouraged by this. One can come to only one conclusion: God was calling him. Again, I wish we had asked him more questions. That we did not was no doubt because he was indeed just Dad. What he did we simply took for granted.

First on his mind was earning enough to send for his mother and two younger brothers, Albert and John. In a year, by careful saving and a little borrowing, he was able to send for them.

One of the activities that Harm enjoyed in the church he had joined, First Christian Reformed Church of Chicago, was singing. He attended their choral society. So did the Kuiper sisters, including my mother, Nellie. The Kuipers had come from Rotterdam. Their father, Homme, or Homer, had been a sail maker, as his father before him. When my mother was fourteen years old, he passed away. He had contracted tuberculosis of the spine.

As he lay dying, he sang the words of Psalm 17, the song that is number 31 in our English Psalter:

> When I in righteousness at last,
> Thy glorious face shall see;
> When all the weary night is past,
> And I awake with Thee
> To view the glories that abide,
> Then, then I shall be satisfied. (Psalter 31:7)

Many times, after we sang that number in church, Mom would remind me of that story.

My mother had just finished eighth grade and graduated with

honors, having been awarded a silver watch for her diligence. Now she had to quit school and go to work to help support the family. How she regretted it! She compensated for it by becoming an avid reader. Whenever she sat in her wing chair in the living room of an evening, it was with a book on her lap and a pair of knitting needles in her hands, for she could read and knit at the same time.

The Kuipers did not all emigrate at the same time. Svann (Sadie) came first, in 1905. She was the independent one. At a time when few women went to college, she received a master's degree in education from the University of Michigan and for many years was a beloved teacher in Manhattan, Montana. Then she abruptly retired to a few acres of land near Ada, Michigan. Later with the help of my oldest brother, Herm, she built a kind of hut into the side of a hill, and there she lived. I never knew why she chose this way, and I do not know if my mother knew either.

The Kuiper sisters in the Netherlands: Christine, Hilda, Sadie, Nellie, Jenny

Kuiper family (1927)
Back: Sadie, George, Nellie,
Christine, Jenny
Front: Grandma, Govert, Hilda

My mother, Pietsche (Nellie), came next with Jansje (Jenny) on the *Nieuw Amsterdam*, in November 1906. Their mother, Janke (Jeanette), my maternal grandmother, came last, with Hiske (Hilda) and Sjoerd (George), and Christine, the three youngest children. The oldest, Govert, stayed in the Netherlands, in Rotterdam, where he was a journalist.

The Kuiper family settled in Chicago and also attended First Christian Reformed Church of Chicago. They enjoyed singing too and went to that same choral society Dad was attending. (My mother always called it "singing school.") The Kuiper sisters were good seamstresses and dressed well on very little money.

Harm was immediately attracted to Nellie. If you saw a picture of her, it would be easy to see why. It was not only her looks that attracted him, however. She was demure and soft spoken, and she had a quality that Dad always called "*streken.*" I don't know just how to translate that into English, but neither did Dad, for in his vocabulary it always remained a Dutch word. I think perhaps it was a quality that helped her achieve her ends without ever being conscious of it herself. At any rate, before long he was walking her home from church and "singing school" and taking her for an occasional buggy ride.

Such was his plan when the churches of Englewood and First Chicago had a joint picnic; but his pastor, Rev. Breen, asked him at the last minute to give a speech, and he did not want to refuse him. After a half hour of preparation he spoke on "Time." When he finished, he had only a little time left to take Nellie for a buggy ride.

Harm now decided to go to Mrs. Kuiper and ask permission for him to be engaged to Nellie. That was the custom. Nellie's siblings knew that he was coming and why, so when he came up the back steps into the kitchen they were expecting him. Sadie was there doing the family washing and invited him to sit down for a minute. He did—almost in her tub of washing. When she screamed, she alerted the whole household. When he got to the parlor, it was to the tune of smothered giggles. My maiden Aunt Jenny loved to tell this story. I never knew whether or not this incident was planned, but I suspect it was.

Courtship days

Permission was duly granted, and Harm and Nellie were officially engaged. They then had a formal engagement picture taken, as was the custom. It was

29

to be a long engagement, for seven years of school faced him before he could fulfill his calling to become a preacher of the gospel.

My mother was destined to have a profound influence on Dad. I never saw him angry with her—impatient, perhaps, but not angry.

Harm and Nellie's engagement picture

Chapter 3

~~~~~

COLLEGE
AND SEMINARY

Harm had very little money saved up to go to college and seminary, for he had used his savings to bring his mother and two younger brothers to America. He never regretted doing this, for he never forgot how his mother had worked long hours to support her little family.

The way to college was not barred. There was a fund provided by the Christian Reformed Church so that aspirants for the ministry could go to college and seminary. In order to qualify, he had to write an essay on the topic "Why I Want to Be a Minister." He divided his subject into two parts: "The Value of It" and "The Urge toward It." He then wrote his essay in Dutch and submitted it. It was accepted, and Harm left for Calvin College and Seminary in the fall of 1908.

He found lodging with the Drukkers, a kindly couple who lived in southeast Grand Rapids near Oakdale Christian School, within walking distance of Calvin College. He enjoyed his days there along with several other students, some of whom were also planning to go into the ministry. They engaged in a good deal of horseplay in their free time.

In those days many of the students were smokers, and so was Harm. One day the students decided to ban all smoking at the boarding house for a month. Harm was the heaviest smoker, but he said he would go along with the plan. When the month was over, Harm went to his room, shut the door, and was not heard from for an hour. At the end of the hour he opened his door and invited his fellow students to come in. The air was blue with smoke. He told them, "That was to show you that I could still smoke." And he smoked all of his life, cigars and a pipe. He always said that he did not inhale, but when you are in a room that is blue with smoke, how can you help inhaling?

Now he could study literature, including poetry and drama, and he drank it all in. He learned foreign languages: French, German, Greek, Latin, and Hebrew. He became proficient in English, even teaching an English class for Prof. Jacob Vanden Bosch. He wrote a play in Dutch; he had been assigned by his English professor to write one act of a play, but once he started, he wrote a complete play and sold it to his friend William Eerdmans for ten dollars.

The name of the play was *Dominie Kouwenaar.* It was about a young, unmarried preacher who is dating a young girl from his congregation. When she tells him she is pregnant, they agree to hide his involvement, and she bears the shame alone. The problem arises when a mysterious *voddenrapper* (ragman) appears from time to time and hints of his involvement.

It was published some time later, when Dad was in his first pastorate at Fourteenth Street Christian Reformed Church in

Holland, Michigan, and Dad was a little embarrassed to see it in the home of one of his parishioners. He was not a fan of drama when I was growing up. We were not permitted to attend the school plays. His reasoning was that no one could act sin, and neither could he act holy things.

Harm found ways to supplement his livelihood by teaching Dutch and English to his fellow students. When he taught it, it was not only the vocabulary, but also the grammar, the spelling, and the diction. He taught Dutch to the children of Dennis Avenue Christian Reformed Church, because their minister could teach catechism only in Dutch and their parents wanted them to understand what they were learning. Some of these children later became his parishioners and recalled how he used to carry them on his shoulders and engage in horseplay at recess.

At one point he worked for the Grand Rapids Public Library for six cents an hour.

The days passed quickly, and after one year he returned to Chicago to work for the Aermotor Windmill Company and replenish his funds. He also wanted to see his Nellie and apparently to persuade her family to move to Grand Rapids, for that is what they did.

Harm had heard a covenant view that he simply could not accept and certainly could not teach. It had been taught in a course in Reformed doctrine by Prof. William Heyns. Professor Heyns had taught that the covenant promise was for all the children of believers, on condition that they would believe. Harm's Reformed nature rebelled against any teaching that would make God's work dependent on man. If that was the official teaching of the church, he could not be a preacher in that church.

He consulted Rev. Klaas Kuiper, an old friend, who advised him to take time to study the matter and not to act hastily. That is what he did. It became the most important study of his life.

Dad in Flat Creek, NY, in 1913

When Harm went back for his second autumn in Grand Rapids, he chose to share a room with a fellow student, not far from where Nellie and her family had found a place, for they had indeed moved to Grand Rapids. He lived on Sherman Street; she lived nearby on Dolbee Street. Nellie had found work at the Stickley Brothers Furniture Company. Harm, now known as Herman, met and walked her home every day. The work she did was hard, and Nellie turned over all her earnings to her mother, who gave her bus fare. When she and Herman were married, she had not a cent to call her own.

Herman did chores for the Kuipers, for Nellie's youngest brother George had stayed in Chicago, and there were some chores better suited for a man. In return he ate his meals with the Kuiper women and also taught them English. He did not simply teach them to speak the language, but he also taught them written English, together with its grammar and spelling. My mother Nellie learned her English from him too. After my parents had passed away, we found some of those handwritten lessons in a drawer. They were not easy. The vocabulary was not made up of words you might use every day; often they were three and four syllables long.

After World War II, when many letters came from her relatives in the Netherlands, my mother sometimes found it difficult to answer them. She had learned her English well but had forgotten some of her Dutch. In spite of this she never lost her Dutch accent. We used to tease her sometimes that her "veils" were "whales" and her "whales" were "veils."

Herman had now entered the seminary. From the time he was licensed to preach, it became his chief joy. He loved to get on the pulpit. He preached in both Dutch and English. Few of the seminary students could do this, and when the seminary received a request for someone to go to Flat Creek, New York, and preach in English for the summer, Herman was asked to go. Flat Creek was a church located in the Mohawk River Valley near Canajoharie, New York. It was not a Christian Reformed church, but the people knew of Calvin College and Seminary

Many years later, when we were on our way to the East Coast for a family vacation, we came through Canajoharie on the New York Thruway. Abruptly Dad said, "I'd like to stop in Flat Creek." We turned off the thruway and soon came to a little settlement. Dad went up to a screen door and knocked, at the same time calling, "Is anyone here?" A woman came outside, wiping her hands on her apron, and exclaimed, "I know that voice; that's Rev. Hoeksema!" Needless to say, we were pretty impressed. Dad had been there last in 1914; we were now in the 1930s.

On June 7, 1914, my parents were married. Prof. Louis Berkhof married them; Nellie's youngest sister, Christine, and her fiancé, Anthony Vander Meer, were their attendants. Herman and Nellie spent that summer in Flat Creek, for the seminary had asked Herman to go there again. When they returned, they moved to an apartment above Trompen's Dry Goods Store on Eastern Avenue. There Johanna Dorothy, their first child, was born on June 16, 1915. They named her Johanna after Dad's mother. I do not know why her middle name was Dorothy; they probably just liked the name. The same month Herman graduated from seminary, and shortly afterward he became eligible for his first call to a congregation.

Marriage certificate of Herman and Nellie

Wedding picture of Herman and Nellie

Dad, Mom, and first baby Johanna

Chapter 4

❧

FOURTEENTH STREET CHRISTIAN REFORMED CHURCH

Dad was now ready for his first charge. Where would God send him?

He received several calls; he was inclined to go to Paterson, New Jersey. Why that call appealed to him, I do not know; perhaps because it was near the ocean. But that is only speculation. He knew too that Fourteenth Street in Holland was vacant and that he had been added to that church's original trio when some of its members demanded it; and then he had received the call. Dad knew the weak reputation of that congregation regarding strong Reformed doctrine and Christian education, and he asked to meet with them. He told the congregation what they could expect from him. They would hear strong, doctrinal, Reformed preaching and emphasis on Christian education. And he told

Fourteenth Street CRC in Holland, MI,
Dad's first charge

them to shake hands with him if they still wanted him to come. It was like saying, "You don't really want me here, do you?"

But almost everybody shook his hand, and he knew God was sending him to Fourteenth Street. That is what he told Nellie when he came home. And so to Fourteenth Street the three of them went: Dad, Mom, and Jo, a little dark-haired toddler of about two.

From the beginning he found a few practices that he did not expect. Fourteenth Street had a choir, and the minister was accustomed to entering with the choir instead of with the consistory. I do not know how long Dad kept up that practice, if at all. Another practice he had not anticipated was that the young people did not meet for Bible discussion in a society, but had followed the practice of the Reformed Church of America and had become a part of Christian Endeavor, a non-denominational evangelical organization whose goal is to bring youth to accept Christ and to work for him. These were relatively minor skirmishes. His bigger battle was over the Christian school.

I often wonder why Christian education seems to be such a big issue. Is it a question of money? I hardly think so, because some of the most generous souls are sometimes opposed to Christian education. Is it a matter of not wanting to be distinctive, a soldier of the cross? Perhaps. Whatever it was, some of Dad's fiercest opposition at Fourteenth Street was over the Christian schools.

Not everyone, by any means, was opposed to Christian education. Many in the congregation were completely behind it. Perhaps the opposition was more vocal; that often happens.

Dad followed the good custom of family visitation every year, and he always asked for a volunteer elder to go with him. The same ones always volunteered, and he knew that the others were not behind some of his preaching and methods. He told the elders who supported him not to volunteer the next time he asked for an elder to go with him, and so when he asked, he was met with silence. Finally he said, "If no one will go with me, I'll ask for some new elders." He got his reluctant elder. It was certainly an unorthodox way to deal with the problem, but it achieved the necessary result.

Dad faced every problem head on, and the result was that it sharpened the differences that existed in the congregation. Some there were whose Reformed faith was strengthened and who became loyal followers of the truth. Some became more vocal in their opposition and began to talk about finding another place to worship. That brought sadness and worry to some that the congregation was going to be drastically diminished. Dad did not hold back. Rather, his preaching became stronger.

I can understand now something he used to say about the preaching of the word being one of the keys of the kingdom: it was a matter of strengthening the faith of some and of being uncompromising in the preaching of the truth, so that the preaching was so unpalatable that the opposition would leave. The preaching would be strong, even stronger as the objections increased, so that he would "preach them out of the church"—or they would change and believe the truth that was preached. That is what happened at Fourteenth Street: the strong became stronger; the weak left. It was the exercise of the keys of the kingdom.

Then World War I broke out. Feelings ran high against all things German, in the church as well as in the community. Many forgot that God had his church in Germany too. Dad was as pro-American as anyone, but he did not believe that the church was national and therefore did not believe that an American flag belonged in church during a worship service. A flag could be at a program perhaps, but not in a worship service. There was no flag in Fourteenth Street. Newspaper articles, letters, and opinions went back and forth in the *Daily Sentinel*, Holland's newspaper, either critical or supportive of his position.

Threats to Dad's safety began to come. He was threatened with being tarred and feathered. Because of that, he began to carry a .38-caliber revolver and let it be known that he was carrying it. Later he told us about seeing some figures huddled in some bushes when he was walking home one day. He spoke into the bushes: "I have a gun, and I will use it." The figures disappeared. Dad's gun was never fired. Dad never spoke about those days as if he were afraid, but he must have feared for his wife and little girl.

Incidentally, Dad always kept that gun between the upper and lower bookcases in his study when we lived on Franklin Street. We knew it was there, but we never touched it. After he passed away, it went to his oldest son Herman, who gave it to his oldest son Herman.

Dad and Mom with Johanna and Jeanette

About this time a second little girl was added to the Hoeksema family. Blonde, blue-eyed Jeanette Evelyn was born on August 1, 1917. She was named Jeanette for Mom's mother and Evelyn for Dad's sister Everdiene.

The war ended. Holland was now in the throes of the flu epidemic. Many sickened and died. My mother made soup, and Dad brought it to the homes where there was sickness. Sometimes he built a fire there, for there was no central heating in those days. One could not simply turn up the thermostat. Neither Dad nor Mom ever became sick themselves.

Dad was at Fourteenth Street Christian Reformed Church for four and a half years. It was a busy time. He had been involved in denominational work. He had been a delegate to the synod of 1918, where the well-known Bultema case was treated.

Rev. Bultema had been minister at First Christian Reformed Church in Muskegon. He was teaching that Christ was head of his church but king of the Jews, and he would come back to reign

43

over them in Palestine for a thousand years before his final coming. He had written a book called *Maranatha* that embodied this teaching.

The consistory of his church brought a protest against Rev. Bultema to the synod of 1918; it was put into the hands of an advisory committee, which gave a majority and a minority opinion. The synod then appointed a special committee that was to come with a recommendation. Dad was on this committee. He was able to show that Bultema was wrong in saying that Christ was the king only of the Jews and not of his church. He was not going to come back and reign over the Jews for a thousand years. The synod adopted the committee's report.

At this time during his first charge, Dad typed his sermons exactly as he planned to preach them. This was entirely different from what he did in later years, when he took a sheet of unlined paper, folded it in half like a book, made a broad outline, and after studying it, left it home.

Dad developed much in Fourteenth Street, perhaps most of all in his view of the covenant, and that was to be the cornerstone of his theology over the years. He loved series preaching. He studied his sermons until they became almost a part of him. When I knew him, he did this while pacing the floor of his study or if the weather was pleasant, while taking a walk. If I offered to go with him, he gently refused, saying he had to study. Whether pacing the floor in his study or taking a walk, he sometimes referred to this as "learning on the hoof." He never did this on Saturday. That was a family day, and we often went to the beach, weather permitting, or to a park for a picnic. But that was later.

He had been a strong follower of Abraham Kuyper, and he still admired him but did not follow him blindly. He began to question very tentatively Kuyper's theory of common grace, because he could not reconcile it with scripture. He did not presume to be wiser than Abraham Kuyper, but he was searching for a way to prove him to be in harmony with God's word and could not find it.

Now Dad received a call from Eastern Avenue Christian Reformed Church, a large church in Grand Rapids, and he was inclined to accept it. After four and a half years at Fourteenth Street, he felt that God was sending him to this new congregation.

At this time Dad was beginning to separate his teaching from the traditional view of the covenant as an agreement between God and man, consisting of a condition, a promise, and a penalty. When I attended the Christian school in the 1930s, that was the teaching I received. Dad knew that he could have nothing of any tenet that would make man to be a party with God in his own salvation. Many times from the pulpit I heard Dad say, "Man has a part in the covenant: to love the Lord his God. Man is not a party."

While still at Fourteenth Street, Dad had a brief encounter with his former professor, William Heyns, who had just written a book entitled *Manual of Reformed Doctrine*. Professor Heyns, you will recall, was the professor whose covenant view had troubled Dad so much that he almost gave up studying for the ministry. He asked Dad what he thought about the book. Dad thought briefly, then replied, "With your thought, Professor, you do not save one reprobate, and you don't build up the elect. Under my preaching, the elect are instructed, and the reprobate are not deceived that they have an imaginary heaven." Professor Heyns was angry, but Dad had finally spoken the words that he had been searching for, words that spelled out his feeling on the doctrine of the covenant. It was the beginning of a lifelong study that would be shadowed in controversy.

Years before, when he was still in seminary, he had heard

this same teaching, taught even then by this same professor, and already then he knew that he could never believe and teach it. Dad always referred to it as "Heynsian." It had troubled him so deeply that if he were expected to preach this doctrine, he would not have been able to enter the ministry. With all of his being he knew that "salvation is of the Lord."

And so ended his ministry at Fourteenth Street, a charge of which both my father and my mother always spoke fondly.

Chapter 5

EASTERN AVENUE CHRISTIAN REFORMED CHURCH AND DR. JANSSEN

Dad had been at Fourteenth Street for four and a half years when he received the call to Eastern Avenue Christian Reformed Church in Grand Rapids. He was moved to go there. In early 1920, my parents bade a fond farewell to the saints at Fourteenth Street and left for Grand Rapids.

Eastern Avenue was a good-sized congregation. The church was busy building a new parsonage, and soon my parents would be moving again. Their third child was due in a couple of months.

About this time Dad's younger brother John passed away. John was kind of a dreamer; he lived alone in an apartment on Dolbee Street, repaired watches, and played the accordion. The funeral was in Eastern Avenue's parsonage.

Herman Junior (Junior was his middle name) was born on March 21, 1920. My mother became weaker with the birth of

Eastern Avenue church and parsonage, Grand Rapids, MI

*Uncle John on the porch playing
the accordion*

*Johanna, Jeanette,
and Herman Junior*

each child, and Dad urged her to get full-time help in the house. Providentially she heard of Etta Kooistra. Etta lived on Baxter Street with her old father and crippled brother, Simon. That brother owned a small shoe store where he also did shoe repairs. Etta made a home for both of them. Her fiancé had died in the flu epidemic that followed World War I. Etta never lived with us or stayed overnight but came every day. She walked to our house, but when we had a car, Dad took her home. She worked for the family until my father passed away in 1965, and then she voluntarily helped me until her death in 1973. She was always a dear friend.

She was totally loyal. There were times when some out of curiosity would ask her about some little detail of life in the parsonage, but they could get no information out of Etta. She told me this once with a little grin.

Once when one of the neighbor playmates asked if Etta was our maid, I went to my mother with the question. She replied, a little more indignantly than I thought was necessary, "Don't ever call Etta a maid. She is Mother's helper." Even long after I was married, Etta would come and help me too. If we were leaving on a camping trip and Etta got wind of it, she would call and tell me not to clean the house, not to make the beds, and not to do the dishes. She would do it while we were away, despite the fact that she had no transportation besides her two feet. And she often came and helped me with spring cleaning. (We still did that.)

She had few of the ordinary comforts of life. She had a stove in her kitchen with a long pipe coming out of it; that stove must have heated her house. She wanted no luxuries. She did not even have a refrigerator, but she kept some things cold by putting them in her basement. That basement was not a full one; I think they called it a Michigan basement. When our family outgrew its original refrigerator and we bought a new one, I tried to give her the old one, which was still only a few years old. How she agonized over that! Finally she said, "No, I mustn't have it; it wouldn't be good for me." And she went on canning her eggs, never having anything really cold, never having any ice.

One day her brother Si did not come home when Etta expected him. He had had a stroke in his store. They took him to St. Mary's Hospital, and she sat by his side many days, until he passed away. Then she grieved for him for a long time.

She would never let me pay her. The most I could do was to give her my leftovers. Sometimes when she was about to leave, she would ask, *"Hep je ook resjes?"* ("Have you any leftovers?") Then she would go home with my wastepaper and any leftovers and call me to say, "I put the wastepaper in the stove in my kitchen and right away I have a nice fire. And it makes me feel so thankful!"

She tolerated absolutely no levity when it came to anything remotely connected to church or any religious topics. Then she would say, "You must not talk so lightly about such things." Only once could I get her to come for Sunday dinner with Dad; that was after my mother had passed away. It was such a rarity that I took her picture, unbeknownst to her.

The only known picture of Etta Kooistra

One day when she planned to come, she did not show up. I was in contact with her cousin, and we had to authorize the police to break into her house. Etta had passed away. She must have had a stroke and then quickly gone home to be with her Lord. Rev. Cornelius Hanko spoke at her funeral service. His text was Revelation 14:13: "Blessed are the dead which die in the Lord from henceforth: Yea, saith the Spirit, that they may rest from their labours; and their works do follow them." She often told me that she had been helping my mother since my older brother was a baby. That would be fifty years. But back to my story.

Already when he was at Fourteenth Street, Dad had been on the Curatorium, the Board of Trustees, of Calvin College. That board had come with judgments about the quality of the teaching of the professors at the college and seminary, commenting that it was often dull. There was one exception. The board said that the teaching of Dr. Janssen was not dull, but rather thoughtful and interesting. That angered the other professors, who accused Dr. Janssen of sometimes teaching scripture as not being the word of God. They brought that accusation to the Board of Trustees, who told the professors that they should talk to Dr. Janssen first. This was in 1919.

The four professors appealed to the synod of 1920. There they were given a hearing, and there Dr. Janssen was allowed to defend himself. The synod decided that it had "not become evident that Dr. Janssen's instruction was in conflict with the Reformed faith." The four professors then published a pamphlet (in Dutch) titled in English *The Point at Issue in the Janssen Case*.

Dad had been following the case. He was editor of the rubric "Our Doctrine" in the *Banner* at that time and criticized synod for reaching a negative conclusion. He asserted that it was due to a lack of proper examination on synod's part.

He proceeded to investigate the matter himself and collected a goodly amount of student notes, which he carefully examined. Other students came to him to discuss the issue. The four professors came back to the Board of Trustees, and this time it appointed a committee to investigate more closely. Dad was on it. So was Rev. Henry Danhof of First Christian Reformed Church in Kalamazoo, Michigan.

The members of the committee investigated the matter individually for several months, then came together to discuss the issues. They were divided in their opinion, four to three. Dad was on the committee of the majority; so was Rev. Danhof. Their conclusion was that Dr. Janssen failed to treat scripture as the inspired, infallible word of God, and that he taught evolution rather than creation.

Dr. Janssen would not cooperate with the committee, but began to write in the church papers, putting forth his views there. So did Dad, showing that Janssen did not hold to the literal teaching about creation in the book of Genesis. Janssen's starting point was man, not God. Evolution, rather than divine revelation, was the conclusion to which he came. Dr. Janssen did not reply to the charge brought by the committee, but instead attacked Dad's growing conviction that there was no room in Reformed thought for the doctrine of common grace.

The synod of 1922 studied the reports and adopted the majority report. Then they relieved Dr. Janssen of his professorship at Calvin seminary. In spite of all this history, Dad always remained on friendly terms with him. Even in discussing him much later, he never said a negative word about him as a person.

Not so the Janssen supporters. They, following Janssen himself, never discussed the charges against him, charges of teaching evolution rather than creation, of starting with man rather than God. Rather, they too attacked Dad's growing conviction that to teach common grace was not biblical. Two men stood with him against his accusers. One of them was Rev. Danhof of Kalamazoo. The other was Rev. George Ophoff of Hope Christian Reformed Church in Riverbend, Michigan. The latter remained faithful all his life; he taught for many years in the Theological School of the Protestant Reformed Churches and wrote faithfully in the *Standard Bearer*, the magazine published by the Reformed Free Publishing Association.

Two new publications appeared on the ecclesiastical scene. One, *Religion and Culture*, advocated a soft-pedaling of the antithesis between the church and the world. The other, the *Witness*, sought to be distinctively Reformed. On its staff were Prof. L. Berkhof, Prof. S. Volbeda, Rev. H. J. Kuiper, Rev. D. Zwier, Rev. Y. P. De Jong, Rev. H. Hoeksema, and Rev. H. Danhof. Its subtitle was *A Monthly Publication in the Interest of the Reformed Faith*.

In the first issue of the *Witness*, Professor Berkhof wrote an article entitled "Conservative or Progressive." In the article "Is Calvin Losing Its Distinctiveness?" Rev. H. J. Kuiper raised doubts about the spiritual life of the church of that day. Dad wrote most of the meditations in the *Witness*. He also wrote a column entitled "Views on Scripture." In it he explained the principles of scriptural interpretation.

These were days of strong interest in all the questions that arose about doctrine. There were no television, no radio, and few cars. What did people do? They read, studied, were creative, spent time outdoors, and did a lot of discussing together.

In an article that appeared in *Onze Toekomst* (Our future), Dr. Van Lonkhuizen from Chicago defended Dr. Janssen, calling Rev. Danhof and Rev. Hoeksema "hard and unfair men, sons of Zeruiah." (Zeruiah, you recall, was the father of Joab, who was King David's captain and often took things into his own hands.) When Dad replied, he signed himself "One of Zeruiah's Sons."

Dad with Homer

In 1923 on January 30, another boy was born to the Hoeksemas. They named him Homer Cooper. Homer was after Mom's father, Homme. Cooper was a take-off on my mother's maiden name, Kuiper. Each time my mother had a child she took longer to recover. She was thankful she had Etta.

Meanwhile, Dad's busy life in his Eastern Avenue congregation did not slacken. He enjoyed the work and loved to preach and teach. He began a post-confession class, where he taught much about scripture and the confessions. He taught this well-attended class for many years, almost until his death in 1965.

He also wrote articles for the *Witness* and did some denominational work, but he still had time for his family. He took his little girls along on his walks downtown, stopping for ice cream at the Caramel Kitchen. He played jacks with them on the landing to the upstairs. My oldest sister, Jo, had memories of those times. Dad was not very good at jacks. His fingers were thick and clumsy, probably from his many years as a blacksmith. He was no match for those little girls.

Dad's preaching was always strong. One day three men came to his door, objecting to some of his preaching and writing. He told them they belonged at the consistory. When they went there, they accused Dad of public sin. The consistory placed the three under censure when they refused to retract their accusation.

There were other protests against Dad's preaching that went

to classis. Although the protests had not been sent to the consistory of Eastern Avenue, the classis sent them on to the synod of 1924. The synod dealt with these protests, even though they had not been treated in consistory or classis. Moreover, they dealt with them without giving Dad the opportunity to speak in his own defense. Such "justice" does not occur even in the world. Only after he pleaded with the synod to allow him to speak just once, and then he would not ask again, did they allow him to speak.

The result was the formulation of the three points of common grace. The synod did not ask Dad or Rev. Danhof to subscribe to them. They did not ask them to confess to any error. Synod declared the ministers "fundamentally Reformed with a tendency to one-sidedness." They stood uncondemned. That is how synod left the matter, and then they adjourned.

Chapter 6

❧

A NEW BEGINNING

When the synod adjourned, three members and a minister were still under censure at Eastern Avenue Christian Reformed Church for accusing their minister of public sin. Because the synod had failed to accuse their pastor of anything, the consistory asked those men to retract their accusation. They refused. Classis then demanded that Dad's consistory lift its censure. Basing their refusal on synod's decision, the consistory refused. After all, these men had accused their pastor of public sin, and the synod brought no accusation at all.

Then the classis demanded that Eastern Avenue's pastor subscribe to the three points of common grace. The consistory said that was unjust and hierarchical, for synod had demanded nothing of them.

Nonetheless, classis deposed Dad and his consistory in 1924. The consistories of Kalamazoo (Rev. Danhof) and Hope (Rev. Ophoff) signed an Act of Agreement with Eastern Avenue's consistory and called themselves the "Protesting Christian Reformed Churches."

Ninety-two members of Eastern Avenue's congregation who did not agree with Dad and his consistory appealed to the courts for the property. The court ruled that until the matter was settled the majority could stay and worship there. There was a lengthy court trial over the property. Apparently the congregations of Hope and Kalamazoo did not have to go to court over rightful possession of their properties.

The protesting churches started a theological school, and both Dad and Rev. Danhof were its instructors. It was a decisive step for the future of these churches. They must have had no hope of reconciliation, and they were farsighted.

Dad had many invitations to speak, both in Grand Rapids and in the Midwest—Iowa, Illinois, Wisconsin, and the Chicago area. He also wrote much in the *Standard Bearer*, which the Reformed Free Publishing Association began to publish in 1924. When you think of his work load, you wonder how it was possible that he did not collapse under it. Yet God sustained him; it was his own cause he was sustaining.

Dad kept his readers informed about what was happening in the churches in Grand Rapids. He did this in the *Standard Bearer*, under the heading "Amice Fraterque" (Friend and brother).

I was born on August 17, 1925. I was named Lois Eunice, after Timothy's mother and grandmother. My nickname was "the trouble baby." (My parents took delight in reminding me of this.)

Shortly afterward Rev. Danhof and his two nephews, Rev. Ben Danhof and Candidate Ralph Danhof, abandoned the cause to go their independent ways. It was another trial.

Before either group received notice of the court's decision regarding the Eastern Avenue property, it appeared in the *Grand Rapids Press*. The court awarded the church property to the smaller group of ninety-two members. That group immediately installed new locks on the doors, and as a result, the remaining eight hundred members walked in the snow to Franklin Community House on Christmas morning to worship. Assuming that in those days most of the members lived within walking distance of Eastern Avenue church, it must have been a long, cold walk to Franklin Community House, at least a mile away. Yet, full of enthusiasm, their hearts were trusting.

The members of the congregation wasted no time in buying property on the corner of Franklin Street and Fuller Avenue to build a church and parsonage. They obtained the use of the St. Cecilia Building for their worship services. They rented a temporary parsonage on Sherman Street, and my parents lived there until January 1927, when they moved into the new one at 1139 Franklin Street. On the first Sunday in April 1926 the people worshiped in the basement of the new church.

Lois Eunice

Dad and Mom with Lois

First Protestant Reformed Church

These were days of enthusiasm and strong commitment to the truth, of knowing that the cause was God's and that it would prevail. I did not experience any of this early history, of course, but it was related to me. Again the families walked or shared rides. I find it strange that I never asked and no one ever talked about that part of history.

The new building was dedicated on December 22, 1926. The program was in the Dutch language. The next evening a similar program took place in the English language. Each program had three speeches.

Dad literally loved to preach; it was the joy of his life. There were thirteen hundred seats in the auditorium of First Protestant Reformed Church. For many years there was no microphone, but everyone could hear him clearly. I think the first microphone appeared when the congregation called Rev. Richard Veldman to be its second pastor in 1939.

It was not until June 1926 that synod met again and considered the appeal of Eastern Avenue's consistory against the deposition of its consistory and pastor. At this time synod rejected that appeal, and there was no more recourse. Now it was time to look only forward. There was much work to be done.

The young denomination had to have a name. There were two suggestions: Reformed Protestant and Protestant Reformed. Protestant Reformed was chosen. The congregation that met on the corner of Fuller Avenue and Franklin Street was the First Protestant Reformed Church. It is still the same congregation with the same name, but now it meets in a newer church building at 2800 Michigan NE in Grand Rapids.

Protestant Reformed churches were organized all over the Midwest and later in California and Montana. These churches were organized into classes, then after some years into a synod as the churches grew. The work of the churches expanded. Her needs continued to grow. God always saw to it that those needs were met and always raised up young men to preach the truth in the churches and on the mission field. Through the printed page and the radio program the *Reformed Witness Hour*, the truth spread. Decades later book publishing began. Through all these means God brought his own cause forward until it spread throughout the world, always small, but there. Through active mission work in Northern Ireland the church took root there also. And that church in turn has contacts throughout all of Europe. Beginning with contacts in Singapore in the 1970s, a church was established on that island. Recently a denomination of churches has been established in the Philippines.

I have often thought that Dad would be amazed if he could see the situation of the Protestant Reformed Churches, its sister churches, and missions today. The churches are still small, but scattered over the world, thanks to the grace of God in giving many of our leaders the ability to write and to publish the good news of the gospel of grace, and thanks to the opportunity to travel almost anywhere in the world.

It was 1929 when my father revisited the Netherlands. He went alone, without my mother, because he knew she had Etta to help with the family and household. My mother had no wish to go there. She had nothing but bad memories of her voyage to America. She had been so seasick that she had no intention of getting back on that ocean. So Dad bade her farewell and left the day after the church picnic in June 1928. I remember all of the congregation shaking hands with him at that picnic and saying, *"Goede Reis, Dominie."* I did not understand what it was all about; I was just three years old.

Besides his Nellie, Dad wrote each of his five children a note nearly every day while he was sailing across the ocean. He probably was a little homesick. I did not know of these very tender letters until many years later. They appear in this book in the appendix.

Why did he go? I cannot say for sure, but I always thought he was hoping to see his father, and hoping too that he would be changed. If that was true, Dad was disappointed, because he found his father in a saloon. He would not come out to see Dad or talk to him, and Dad did not go in. He did see his Uncle Lulof, however. I have no idea if there were any of his mother's relatives besides this uncle. Dad never talked about any.

Dad had made contact with the Sovereign Grace Union, an

On the Aquitania, *en route to the Netherlands*

organization in London, England. He visited that organization and preached for them on a Sunday. His friendship with the Sovereign Grace Union continued for a good many years. We used to get novels from them. They were not necessarily classics, but they were wholesome and welcome, and for a good while the younger members of the family had some reading material when they had not visited the library.

Sometime later, in the 1930s, a letter came with a black band around the envelope, and Dad immediately said, in rather a sad voice, "Uncle Lulof died." I thought of the song "A Letter Etched in Black." My sisters used to sing it in the car sometimes when we traveled. Sending a letter with a black band around it upon the death of a loved one was still the custom in the Netherlands in those days.

Life went on. These were depression years. Dad asked the consistory to cut his salary. Some in the congregation were losing their homes; we had a roof over our heads. We did not do much Christmas shopping, but nobody did.

In those days we paid our own utilities. The parsonage was heated with a coal furnace, and we bought our own coal in the summer, when it was cheaper. When it came, the company would open our coal chute (it had a heavy metal door) and slide the coal down the chute into the coal bin. Once it was in, Dad would have to shovel it to distribute it a bit. I'm sure they don't make houses with coal bins anymore.

Dad with Uncle Lulof

63

The Hoeksema family, 1928. Notice the expression on the faces of the two children—Homer and Lois—front and center. They had an agreement that they would pull faces whenever they were photographed. My parents never caught on.

We had a gas water heater too, but it had to be turned on; it was not automatic. We heated water in a kettle for washing dishes. I don't remember what we did for baths. We must have turned on the water heater for a while, but we did not have the luxury of a deep, hot bath. We had never had it, so we did not miss it. (I think we could have left the heater on, but that was too expensive, and we paid our own gas bill.)

Every year at Christmas, the Sunday school presented a program to the congregation. The Sunday school was large in those days. The youngest class (I think their ages were from four to six) would sing, and then Dad always had the privilege of chatting with them for a few minutes. They would tell him about their Christmas presents, and then Dad would tell them the Christmas story about the greatest Gift of all.

One Christmas he spotted a little tyke with curls, and on impulse he said, "You have pretty curls; could I have one for Christmas?" After turning to find her mother, and getting her mother's laughing permission, she nodded. Then he heard a chorus of voices, "You may have one of mine too." Dad said with a grin, "All right, if you send me a curl, I will put it in a frame and put it in my study." As the curls came in the mail that year, Dad put them in a large frame and hung them on his study wall.

As a family we did not make much of Christmas with its busy shopping. We did not have a tree until Jo was teaching and bought one for her classroom, then brought it home during the holidays. I soon learned that when my parents lived on Eastern Avenue they had had a tree, decorated with candles, and it had caught fire. Dad had hastily thrown it out of the door, burning his hands in the process. (I always thought that decorating a dry tree with candles was not a very bright idea.)

Later on, when my husband Chuck and I had a tree, my parents came over and enjoyed it with us. For a while we were the only ones of their children who lived in Grand Rapids, and I hated to think of them rattling around in that big house alone, so they would come and enjoy some evenings with our family. (And we put electric lights on our tree.)

I was about five and Homer was seven when we had a difficult bout with scarlet fever. We could have no contact with the outside community, so every night we had to set out our clean bottles, and the milkman would pour milk into them in the morning. (There were no cartons in those days.) My three older siblings had to move out for six weeks while Homer and I were quarantined. We slept in the playroom-sewing room downstairs. My father could hardly abandon his study, so he put heavy cardboard between the French doors at the foot of the stairs, effectively separating the upstairs from the downstairs, or so he thought. But one night we had a cyclone (at least that is what they called it). The doors blew open, the cardboard blew out, and that was the end of the separation. That morning there was a worm in our milk bottle. It must have been a strange wind that could leave the bottle standing and blow a worm into it.

My mother contrived a unique way of bringing meals to my dad. She sent a plate of food on a tray up the clothes chute on a rope for him each day, and he would send his dirty dishes back down the clothes chute via the same rope. She also devised her own way of keeping two active youngsters entertained. We made a quilt. We used plain white muslin and red embroidery floss, and Mom traced large pictures from a bird book on those squares of muslin. We embroidered them in red with a simple backstitch. Then she stitched them together on her sewing machine and later quilted them. I wish I knew what happened to that quilt.

On one of those early spring days, some kind ladies from church brought my brother and me each a box of chocolate bunnies: a real treat! I remember that we opened the windows in the playroom-sewing room to talk to those ladies, and the air was so balmy. We could hardly wait to go outdoors and to have our siblings come home. We had been separated from the rest of the family for five weeks.

At that time I was in the beginners' class in catechism. It was a big class of ages five to seven, taught by one of the seminary students, who had varying abilities when it came to keeping order. That was true of most of the daytime classes; not so much of the beginners' class, but as the age of the students increased, their behavior worsened, depending on the ability of the student teacher. Because those teachers were his students, periodically Dad would quietly open the door and stand there observing the class. A hush would descend upon it that was almost deafening.

Our parents did not teach us our catechism lesson and rarely checked up on us before we left for catechism. In retrospect, I find that rather strange. It isn't that we did not learn our catechism, and I think we always knew it, but we spent very little time at it. I can't say that Chuck and I ever actually taught our children their lessons either, but we certainly asked them their questions.

Dad's discipline of his children was not corporal punishment, as I recall. The most corporal punishment we ever received was a threat, contrary to what Dad himself would have recommended. If I really misbehaved, Dad would say to me, "Must I take you over my knee?" But I never was taken "over his knee." He had what we always referred to as "the look." It is hard to describe, but you would know it if you were the recipient of it. If you had any mischief planned and you received "the look," you would change your mind. Yet you wouldn't call it exactly threatening. It was as if Dad was saying, "I know what you're planning to do. Don't."

What is growing up without pets? Dad did not know anything about pets and their needs. The first pet we had was a cute little brown-and-white puppy. We got a cage for him, and where did we keep the cage? In the basement. We fed him scraps, not puppy food. I am a dog lover, and I still feel sorry for that puppy. He did not live long. I am not sure just what he died of, whether it was the food or loneliness. When that puppy cried, Dad thought it was because he smelled our fried potatoes, so he brought him a plateful, which was not good for him. We got another puppy, and things went the same way.

Once Dad returned from a trip to Iowa with homing pigeons that someone gave him. We had some kind of home for them on the parsonage tin deck. They were smart. Dad would stand in the yard and whistle a peculiar little whistle, and they would seem to come from every direction and land on his arms, his shoulders—wherever—but they made a mess on the tin deck, and they had to go. We never had cats. My parents did not like cats because they did like the birds that came to visit, and the cats were a threat to the birds.

There was also a time when we had rabbits. Homer had a black rabbit that he named Beelzebub; he taught him to walk around the rim of the sandbox. Dad built a sturdy hutch for the rabbits, but one night a German Shepherd demolished the hutch and killed all the rabbits. We had no more pets.

Chapter 7

VACATIONS

Most of the vacations I remember were spent near water. At first we had no car, so some friends of my parents would take us. Sometimes it was Mr. and Mrs. Nick Yonker from Muskegon or Mr. and Mrs. Jacob Vander Wal from Grand Rapids. They were both very kind couples who took us around a lot in our pre-auto days. The first vacation I remember was at a cottage at Lake Harbor, near Muskegon. There were many cottages to rent, and that's just what we did. One year we rented a cottage called India Inn. Another year we rented Peru Cottage. We thought the cottages were rather pleasant, though I probably would not think so today. There was a creek nearby, and there I learned to swim by floating along with the current into Lake Michigan. Dad did not spend the whole week with us; I do not know who drove him. Once or twice we visited the conference grounds there and heard the visiting evangelist.

Rarely did we head for a small inland lake; usually it was Lake Michigan, or near to it. Almost everywhere we went there was

Black Hills with Rev. and Mrs. Verhil, 1928

Dad at Black Hills, 1928

Swimming in Lake Michigan, 1930

The fishing family at Black Lake

Woe unto the bluegills!

water, except for the time that we went to the Black Hills. I do not know who took us there. I think I was around three years old, perhaps younger, because the only thing I remember was being deathly afraid of a whistle that blew every night around eight o'clock. I think it was a curfew.

There was a place between Holland and Lake Michigan where numerous short roads led to the shores of what was then called Black Lake, but now is called Lake Macatawa. Several people from church owned cottages on one of those roads, and for at least one summer we spent a couple of weeks there. I think the cottage belonged to Bert Boerema, who owned a men's clothing store.

Some of our ministers liked to go there too. I still remember hearing Rev. Gerrit Vos and Rev. William Verhil call, as they walked past our cottage down the short road to the water, "Woe unto the bluegills!" only they said, "Voe unto the bluegills!" We got in the habit of quoting them on the few occasions that we went fishing.

Speaking of Bert Boerema, he did not like it that Dad went hatless in the winter. He was convinced that Dad was going to get something bad, like pneumonia, if he did not wear a hat. Dad did not seem to mind wearing a straw hat in the summer, but he never wore a hat in the winter.

At night we read or played games, but Dad was not there very much. He was not one for fishing, at least not in inland lakes and not very often, so he did not spend much time at that cottage. Black Lake was not much good for swimming, and Lake Michigan was hardly within walking distance. He did go fishing for perch off the pier at Ottawa Beach sometimes, but not on that vacation. When he did go, whoever wanted to could go along; but he always went very early, around four o'clock. That was a little early for most of us, although once in a while my brothers would go with him. He would usually come home around noon, and often with a nice catch of perch, which he would clean and my mother would fry for supper. He did not debone them, and I did not like to struggle with the bones, although the perch did taste very good.

Once we had a car, our summers changed. It must have been in 1933 that we went on a trip up north to the Upper Peninsula of Michigan. Our car was a Chrysler Demonstrator, advertised to have free-wheeling, whatever that was. Dad was going to show that quality to us, so at the top of a long hill he put the car in neutral. When he got to the bottom, the engine killed and it would not start. I was scared we were stuck there, but after a brief wait, it started. It was only a flooded carburetor.

When we traveled, we never ate in restaurants. For the first meal, my mother would prepare a dinner in one big pan. She

Dad in the latest swimwear

Dad cleaning the pan with sand

Eating along the roadside on our way out East

Time to eat

wrapped it in towels and blankets to keep it warm. It traveled at her feet until noon, when we would stop in a park or by a lake if we could find one. We washed all of our utensils right away, and if necessary, we washed them better at the end of the day. I do not know what year we bought our first cooler, but I don't think they even made them in the early 1930s. We had to buy what we wanted to eat shortly before we prepared it. I do not remember any such thing as take-out places or fast-food restaurants in those days either.

While we ate no meals in restaurants, Dad was not averse to stopping for an ice cream cone, especially after we began to chant, "Here we sit like birds in the wilderness, waiting to be fed." What happened to our budget I do not know, but we certainly ate well. Sometimes Dad did the cooking, especially if the menu included something like pork chops with potatoes and sweet corn. He obviously enjoyed cooking, but besides that, he was always looking for ways to make Mom's life a little easier.

As the family grew up, our vacations changed, as could be expected. My sisters graduated from college and took teaching jobs—first Jo and two years later Jeanette. Jo married Lambert Doezema in 1938, and Jeanette married Bill Clason in 1942. Herm was married to Annette Doezema in 1940, so we had no more vacations together.

On our first trip to northern Michigan, we took a boat ride on the Tahquamenon River and were thrilled when a black bear swam across the river in front of the boat. We rode the Toonerville Trolley and were summoned by the host of our motel to see a moon rainbow, something we hadn't seen before and have not seen since. We did not have luxuries, but we did not know what they were anyway. It was the first of several trips we took as a family.

My room adjoined my parents' room, and one night I overheard a conversation between them. They must have thought I was sleeping, but I could hear enough of what they said to understand that they were discussing a possible trip to the eastern United States. Dad wanted to drive to the ocean; it was always like a magnet to him. The question was whether or not they had sufficient funds. The figure of $163.00 as their savings persists in my mind.

Swimming at Green Lake, NY, en route to the East coast

That seems impossible, but gas was cheap: sometimes seven gallons for a dollar. The upshot of that discussion was that early one Tuesday morning in July, we left for parts east.

We did not have a definite destination, but we traveled by way of Niagara Falls, spending some time sightseeing there. We had been there before and would go there again, but now we were on our way to the ocean. We went east along the New York Thruway, since freeways were far in the future. There were some three-lane roads, but Dad did not like to drive on them. In those days you almost needed a referee to tell you whose turn it was to pass: yours or that of the oncoming traffic.

We must have crossed Lake Champlain at Burlington, Vermont. Traveling was not nearly so common then as it is today and often could have a personal aspect. The ferryboat's captain talked with us and told us a story as we passed a large pointed rock that jutted up in the middle of the lake. During the War of 1812, he said, an American ship captain had been firing a good share of the night at an enemy ship, or so he thought, without being able to sink it. Finally, as it began to dawn, he exclaimed, "By thunder! It's a rock!" And ever since it had been known as Thunder Rock.

We passed through part of the White Mountains of New Hampshire and the lower Green Mountains of Vermont but avoided the higher Adirondacks of New York, because we were headed for the ocean. We came to it a little north of Boston, Massachusetts, near Gloucester. Actually, we knew that we were approaching the ocean for some time before, for Dad had commented some miles back, "Ah—can you smell the salt air?" We could smell it, all right, but we were unanimous in our dislike of the smell. It took a bit of getting used to.

We found a cottage that would fit all of us, a little north of

Boston, and there we stayed for a few days. It was Thursday and there were a lot of historical sites around Boston: Bunker Hill, Old North Church, Boston Harbor, Lexington and Concord— everywhere we went there was something connected with the Revolutionary War. And we were not far from Philadelphia, with all of its history of the beginning of the United States.

The cottage we rented was not far from the rocky shore of Cape Ann and was owned by a Portuguese lady. She told us, "It's clean, but it doesn't shine." That became a byword. We used it whenever we might have done a less-than-perfect job of cleaning a room, for example. And we always referred to that cottage as "the Portuguese cottage." It was our headquarters when we visited Boston.

Jeanette was our navigator. We needed one, because in those days there were no expressways, and there did not seem to be a straight street in the whole city. Jeanette was doing a good job, but nevertheless, on a whim, Dad picked up one of the many street urchins to be our navigator, a little boy named Frankie. Now we had eight in the car, and the eighth one needed a bath.

Frankie found Bunker Hill and a few other places. When he wanted us to turn, he would crook his finger at a street corner. Finally we were ready to drop him off, and he said anyplace was all right, and so we left him. He could not have had much of a home life. That was another way in which travel was educational, something that Dad always maintained.

We went back to Boston another day. We also went to church there on Sunday, but I do not remember where. Then we headed for Philadelphia, where there were many historical sites, but I do not remember many of them. I must have been barely seven years old. I do know that Dad tried to show us as much as possible. Who knew when or if we would return?

For some reason Dad wanted to spend the next Sunday in

Paterson, New Jersey. Now I know why: his first call had come from Paterson. Where we stayed that weekend I do not know. But what happened after church I will never forget. In church there was a lady from our congregation in Grand Rapids. When she spotted Dad she said to him, "Well, as long as you're going home, I'll just ride with you." She did not ask. She did not even ask if we had room. Dad would certainly have said, "Not really." Apparently Dad did not know how to refuse her.

When he told us, we gave a concerted groan. She was not by any means a petite lady, and we were already so crowded that we had to take turns sitting forward in the back seat. Cars were narrower in those days, and now we had to squeeze five bodies into that back seat.

But we dutifully picked her up the next morning and then headed for home. There was no more sightseeing; I do not know what we did for meals or for cabins at night. I only know that we were glad to pull into our own driveway. So ended our first trip to the East Coast.

We went back to the ocean, but for a different reason. It was probably in 1935 that something happened that was to affect our summers for a few years. I came home one Sunday morning to a very quiet house. Usually Dad would sit down at our old pump organ after church and play a few Dutch chorales. One of our church organists had given him some lessons, and it was enjoyable for him. Now a sort of pall hung over the house, and I had no idea why.

But I soon found out. For the first time in his life, Dad had had an attack of nerves. It happened while he was reading the baptism form. He had read it so often that it became automatic, and he lost his concentration. Because he thought about it and feared that it would happen again, it did. Of course it did. It became a phobia. What had been his chief delight became his fear. It happened only in the preliminaries; once he started to preach, it was gone.

He told his consistory, but they had already known something was wrong and told him to take a long vacation. That is how it happened that we went to Maine that summer. We did not plan to go to Maine, but headed north into Canada for a little trip first. It was our first venture into French-speaking Quebec. Dad seemed to enjoy practicing his French; the rest of us had our difficulties.

In those days my sisters had white straw hats, and they had become soiled. They tried to find some sort of hat cleaner, but could not make themselves understood when they went into a store. Jo pointed to her hat and tried to make a motion of cleaning. The young girl who was the clerk, thinking she understood, said "Shampoo? Shampoo?" Jo replied, "Yes, shampoo for de hat." I don't think she ever found her hat cleaner, but we laughed about that episode for a while.

Those were certainly different days. Who would think of traveling with a white straw hat today, let alone worrying if it got a little soiled? Yet on the few occasions that we stopped to go through one of the many magnificent cathedrals, if my sisters did not wear a hat, the person at the door would stop them and they would take their handkerchiefs and put them on their heads. I do not know at what age a head covering was required, but apparently I was too young to fall into that category.

We visited Montreal and Quebec, saw the historic sites, enjoyed the horse-and-buggy rides, and found an English-speaking church. I don't remember much of it. Then we headed east to the ocean. It was still a long way, and much of it was wilderness. When we came to the coast, we followed it south to Portland,

Maine. We had no definite destination but were looking for a cottage close to the ocean, a place that was quiet, not a busy resort.

In Portland we headed a little east, to find a road that paralleled the coast, in an effort to find a cottage. We went through Old Orchard, a busy resort with many cottages but too many people.

We continued on that road until it ended in a little village called Camp Ellis. At the junction was a general store, and Dad went in to inquire about cottages. The proprietor of the store was Mr. Lewis. I remember his name only because I associated it with the union boss John L. Lewis. Mr. Lewis knew of a cottage to rent, and we could see it from where we waited.

So we drove to where the road turned away from the beach, to a large frame house. The children waited while our parents went in. Just a few minutes later they came out to tell us we were staying there. That was the beginning of a few vacations at Camp Ellis, Maine.

That cottage was large; it had four bedrooms, a living room, large dining area, a kitchen with a woodstove, no running water, a large porch, and an outhouse. I thought my parents were a little hasty in renting it, especially my mother, who left behind not only many conveniences, but also Etta besides. The walls of the outhouse were papered with catalogs. I remember this poem was taped to the wall:

> The trouble I think with us all
> Is the lack of high conceit.
> If each one thought he was sent to this world
> To make it a bit more sweet,
> How soon we would brighten the world;
> How easily right all wrong,
> If nobody shirked, and each one worked
> To help his brother along.

I do not remember the next lines. Then, "Rise up today in your might, and say, I am part of that first great cause." High conceit indeed!

That cottage was owned by two ladies, and we surmised from the literature we found in the house that they were of Christian Science persuasion. They were also fans of E. Phillips Oppenheim, the mystery writer. We did not have to visit the library very often that first year. We gained some knowledge of Christian Science that summer and read novels, often on the beach.

Dad in rowboat with Herm

A little rowboat came with the cottage. It was anchored in the Saco River, which was a long stone's throw from our back door. There was no safety equipment on that boat: no life jackets, no life preservers, nothing. Yet my two brothers went down the Saco River in it day after day into the vast ocean, and we never worried about them. In retrospect I can hardly imagine it, but it's true.

They had to go down the river with the outgoing tide and come back when the tide turned. They usually fished for mackerel, but once they came home with a big lobster. Maybe someone gave it to them. I remember being horrified when my mother put it alive into a kettle of boiling water!

Every morning before breakfast, Dad would go for a swim in the ocean. He usually swam at the same time as a certain Roman Catholic priest, and as they both took walks afterward, they began to walk together. One day Dad decided to ask the priest something about his church. The man replied, "What's that pink spot on your chest?" Dad told us this story when he came home.

When Dad came back from those morning swims, he would sit in front of the woodstove in the kitchen and shiver until he warmed up. Once that priest brought a thermometer with him. When he tested the water, he found it to be forty-nine degrees.

Dad would gradually tan, a deep, reddish-brown tan. I think he was rather proud of that tan—until one day when he was taking a walk down the beach a young lad stopped him and asked, "Hey, mister, are you brown from the sun?" Dad, pleased the boy had noticed, replied, "Yes." The boy put out his hand and said, "Well, I'm Smith from the *Tribune*." Dad told us this story, laughing, when he returned from his walk.

Dad did not paint (one of his most enjoyable hobbies) any pictures at the cottage we rented, but he did find a scenic spot some miles away, and after he found it, he went back there several times to paint, until the picture was close enough to completion that he could finish it at our cottage. That beach faced south, and there was usually a breeze there, resulting in surf. The beach at Camp Ellis faced east, and usually the wind was from the west. We had big rollers, but no surf.

The place where he painted was called Fortune Rocks, and it was not far from a place called Kennebunkport. Two pictures were the fruit of those trips; he gave them to my sisters.

If the weather was chilly or rainy, we usually went for a ride somewhere and explored the countryside. Once, because we had seen so many signs advertising the Desert of Maine, we decided to go there on a cloudy day. We came to a place where the soil was a little sandy, much like you might see as you approach Lake Michigan, and there was a sign with the admission posted on it for the Desert of Maine. I remember my mother was particularly indignant: "If they think I'm going to pay to see someone's overblown farm, they can think again," she said, and we turned around and went back.

Sometimes we would drive to Portland. There were several places of interest there. My mother and sisters liked to shop, and they found a good yarn store that they visited. There was a well-furnished library in Portland too. We found an Orthodox Presbyterian Church there, which we attended. Over the years they had three different pastors, and they all visited us at one time or another.

Dad painting at Fortune Rocks, 1937

Before we found that church, we had sought a place to worship in Biddeford. The church we tried was Congregational, and it was a disaster. I think the minister must have thought he would practice his altar call on us, as we were strangers, because he came out with a particularly rank one: "God doesn't have anything to say about it," he shouted. "It's all up to you." Needless to say, we did not go back there.

Dad had become interested in baseball, particularly the Detroit Tigers. If the Tigers were playing the Boston Red Sox, he would take whoever wanted to go to watch the game. It was a very busy Route One that led there. There were not yet any expressways. My mother never went on those trips to Boston; she did not like the busy road, and she did not especially care about the Tigers either.

It was six miles from our cottage to Saco, the first of the twin cities of Biddeford and Saco; we took a blacktop road to get there. Dad would often walk to Saco, and one of the other drivers in the family would pick him up. Sometimes my mother would ride along and get a few groceries. They often bought cantaloupe: that, with a scoop of ice cream, was our favorite evening snack. Of course we had to buy the ice cream the last minute, from Mr. Lewis's store, because there was no refrigerator or freezer in that antique cottage.

When Dad walked to Saco, he would invite anyone to go along. I did it once, and that was enough. Six miles is a long way to walk when you're only ten years old. My brothers often went with him, and when they did, they always stopped for a sundae, usually at the dime store, which had a good-sized soda fountain. Above that fountain was a picture of a girl who was daydreaming while her ice cream melted and ran down the sides of the glass. My siblings never failed to compare me with that girl, because I was a slowpoke, and invariably they had to wait for me.

I do not know how many years we went back to Camp Ellis, but Jo was married in 1938, and I know we did not go after that. The time away and the fresh air and exercise had certainly helped Dad. He did not speak of that unreasoning fear again, and we did not ask him. But once, many years later, on an impulse I asked him, "Dad, do you still get that nervous feeling on the pulpit?" He responded with a kind of whimsical smile, "I'm too old to be nervous."

Chapter 8

BROUGHT UP SHORT

D ad had always followed closely the events in the church world, particularly the Reformed church world. The church papers from the Netherlands all came to his desk, and he read them carefully. Thus when discussions arose in the Netherlands about such topics as the covenant, the immortality of the soul, self-examination, common grace, the natures of Christ, and others, he commented on them in the *Standard Bearer*, which was exchanged with Dutch magazines. Writers there took note of his comments.

Soon the lines began to be drawn more sharply, particularly between the followers of Dr. Valentine Hepp and Dr. Klaas Schilder of the Netherlands. In 1936 a committee was appointed to try to resolve the differences between the two factions. The committee too was divided, and in 1944 Dr. Schilder was deposed. That was the beginning of the Liberated Churches in the Netherlands.

Dad wrote much in the *Standard Bearer* about the situation, and Dr. Schilder responded. This went on for some time. In

Dad and Mom with Dr. Klaas Schilder, 1939

1939 Dr. Schilder came to the United States for a visit, despite the fact that some Christian Reformed brethren were less than welcoming. The highlight of his visit was a conference for the reunion of the Christian Reformed and the Protestant Reformed churches. Dr. Schilder and Mr. William Eerdmans organized the conference, which was held in the Pantlind Hotel in Grand Rapids. It was attended by sixteen Christian Reformed and fourteen Protestant Reformed ministers, and it was an all-day conference intended to be a step toward reuniting the two denominations.

Dad expected that one of the Christian Reformed brethren would come with some sort of position paper. He had prepared one, and as was to be expected, it was thorough. The others came with nothing. The meeting adjourned with no steps toward reconciliation having been made. Dr. Schilder was bitterly disappointed. Shortly after dinner that evening, the doorbell rang. There stood Dr. Schilder. He said, *"Ik heb de smoor in"* ("I'm sick to my stomach"). This was the first and last serious attempt at reconciliation between the denominations.

In 1940 a delegation from the Young Men's Society came to see Dad. They wanted to start a radio program, and they wanted Dad to be the speaker. Dad was delighted that the young men wanted to take on this project. It was a healthful sign for the church that they were interested, and he enthusiastically agreed. A radio choir was organized too.

At first we went to downtown Grand Rapids to broadcast at the radio station. Then broadcasting was done in First Protestant Reformed Church. Dad would speak from the consistory room, and the choir would sing from the auditorium, near where the piano stood. Still later both the music and the speech were pre-recorded. Eventually the committee was able to purchase its own recording equipment, and both the time and place were unlimited.

The first series that was broadcast was on God. As I recall, some of the titles were "God is God," "God is the Lord," "God is Almighty." That program, still known as the *Reformed Witness Hour*, is heard today over many stations.

In December 1941 the Japanese attacked the United States at Pearl Harbor. That was the begin-ning of a long and bloody World War II. The country fought on two fronts, from the jungles of the South Pacific to the battle-fields of Europe—the young men from our churches too. Dad wrote many letters to the servicemen.

The United States won the victory in Europe, and we cel-ebrated VE Day by going to downtown Grand Rapids. The people were snake-dancing in the

Recording a radio sermon, 1950s

87

streets. I was surprised that Dad let me go, but maybe he thought it had been a tough time for all of the young people; or maybe he didn't realize just how wild it was downtown. Suddenly there were no more shortages of anything: there was plenty of gas, plenty of sugar, plenty of meat. You could find anything you wanted.

The United States was still fighting on the Pacific front. Our biggest fear at that time was that the government was going to send the well-trained army from Europe directly to the South Pacific without a furlough. Before that could happen, the United States government unleashed the atomic bomb, and the war was over. It was a terrible weapon, but it saved the lives of many of our soldiers. Over a little time they came home, but many never did.

I had met Chuck Kregel in my first year (1942) at Calvin College, and we had dated a lot that year. He was drafted in May and soon sent overseas, first to England, then to France and Germany. We wrote frequently but were not committed to each other. He came home in December 1945, and then we dated exclusively.

Dad was always free with Chuck. He liked to have him come over and play a game of Rook. Chuck was always free with him too. He did not grow up in the Protestant Reformed denomination, so he did not have that feeling toward Dad of awe, of distance, that some did, although Dad always said he couldn't figure out why. Chuck soon joined First Church and was an active member in the Protestant Reformed Churches until his illness, serving as deacon and elder until he could do it no longer.

We were married in May 1947. Dad married us in First Church, and after the reception we left on a brief honeymoon. Shortly after we returned, Dad and Mom, with Bill and Jeanette, left for California to visit my sister Jo and Lam, her husband. Chuck and I lived in the parsonage in order to care for and water the garden while Dad and Mom were gone.

The four of them made it to Sioux Falls, South Dakota. They had had dinner, and Dad and Mom were taking a stroll around the grounds, when Dad experienced a sharp pain that was almost overwhelming. They immediately headed back to their room, where Dad collapsed. I do not know the details of how he got to the hospital. I did not ask, because it did not matter. But he had had a heart attack and a massive stroke, and he had lost the ability to walk or talk.

In the providence of God they were directed to an excellent doctor and hospital. One of the family members stayed with him all of the time. Mom asked for Homer to come to Sioux Falls too. They also wired Dad's consistory back home to tell them what had happened. The consistory sent him a gift of a beautiful bouquet of roses and a loving note. Dad was so overcome by this expression of love that he suddenly burst forth into the Dutch version of Psalm 27:13–14:

> *Zoo ik niet had geloofd, dat in dit leven*
> *Mijn ziel Gods gunst en hulp genieten zou,*
> *Mijn God, war was mijn hoop, mijn moed, gebleven?*
> *Ik was vergaan in al mijn smart en rouw.*
> *Wacht op den Heer, godvruchte schaar, houd moed:*
> *Hij is getrouw, de bron van alle goed;*
> *Zoo dealt Zijn krachtop u in zwakheid neer;*
> *Wacht dan, ja wacht, verlaat u op den Heer.*

"I had fainted, unless I had believed to see the goodness of the LORD in the land of the living. Wait on the LORD: be of good courage, and he shall strengthen thine heart: wait, I say, on the LORD." He could not say it again. He could not say anything else either. Truly he had to wait on the Lord. So did we all.

However, one of the Protestant Reformed ministers in the West looked at matters a little differently. He came when Dad could have no visitors as yet, walked into his room and told Dad not to worry, because the other ministers would take over the work. That was enough to take away any incentive Dad might have to get well. My mother was angry and could not get him out of the room fast enough.

And then there was Rev. Gerrit Vos. He was pastor in Edgerton, Minnesota, about sixty miles from Sioux Falls. Almost every day he drove to Sioux Falls just to cheer up the family and spend time with them. How we appreciated him! He did not even ask to see Dad.

After a few days Chuck and I decided that we would like to see Dad too. Homer was already there; Mom had asked him to come. Chuck and I had not yet purchased a car. We took Homer's old car, which was not very roadworthy, and together with Trude, Homer's wife, headed for Sioux Falls. We stayed in the same motel as the rest of the family, and Chuck took his turn sitting with Dad, together with Homer and Bill Clason, Jeanette's husband.

One night, as Chuck was sitting with him, Dad became agitated about something and, of course, could not tell Chuck what it was. Chuck pointed to everything he could think of in an effort to find the cause of Dad's worry. Finally he noticed that the faucet in the sink was dripping, and when he pointed to it, a look of relief spread over Dad's face. That was it!

While we were there, Chuck sold Homer's old car. When the time came for Dad to come home, Homer and Trude, together with my mother and Dad, took the Pullman sleeper train to Chicago; from there my mother and Dad went by ambulance. We took the train too, all the way home. Bill and Jeanette drove Dad's car home.

Chapter 9

❧

RECOVERY

Then began a long therapy. Dad complained bitterly at first, but the therapist knew what she was doing. We followed through at home too, walking with him, first the length of a room, then going from room to room, then walking outdoors (at night, because Dad was self-conscious about using a cane).

He had speech therapy too. He began to see the possibility of getting back on the pulpit someday. Homer and I took turns reading in unison with him. We read articles from the *Reader's Digest* mostly, because they were easy to understand. He even began to read Greek and Hebrew, but Homer had to listen to him do that. Each new achievement was a source of encouragement to him.

The one thing he was never able to relearn was to type. He had taught himself to type many years before, but he used only his thumbs. In spite of that he could type fast and accurately. He had composed at his typewriter too and never revised, which was one reason he could accomplish so much. Now that ability was gone, and it never came back. Whatever kind of work he had previously produced on his typewriter, he now spoke into a wire recorder and sent the reels to Homer, who transcribed them and sent them back; but that was after 1949, when Homer was minister in Doon, Iowa.

The evening came when Dad walked to the corner and back: two long blocks. It was a milestone, and when he returned, it was with a shout of victory.

There were discouragements too. Every year, since its beginning, Dad had given the keynote speech at the Young People's Convention. This year he could not. He had thoroughly enjoyed that privilege, but now he knew that it would not happen. When he heard others talking about the convention, it must have ached a little. Thankfully he eventually did get back to giving that speech.

I don't know just when he learned to drive again, but Homer was the one to teach him. It was a long time before I would let our children ride with him, and when they did, I never felt quite easy. Patience was never one of his virtues, and it showed in his driving.

But now he faced a cold Michigan winter, and he would probably not get much exercise. My parents thought it would be a good idea to visit Jo and Lam in California. There they could walk; there they could be outdoors and escape some of the Michigan winter. There they could visit their grandchildren; there he hoped to gain enough strength to be able to leave his cane behind and walk without it.

So they traveled by train to Bellflower, California. It was a healing time for Dad, but it was a busy time for Jo. Dad went swimming in the ocean. It was another small step in his recovery, and that is what we were all concentrating on at that time.

He did indeed leave his cane in California when he and my mother came home. But he never lost his slight limp, and neither did he lose his consciousness of it. You could tell by the way he walked, and the way he tried to conceal it. And yet he was much stronger when he resumed preaching in 1948.

Often he would refer to himself as a cripple. Meanwhile, my good friend, who had had polio, sat in the front row in church. She could walk only with crutches and great difficulty. One day I said, "Dad, how do you think she feels when you refer to yourself as a cripple?" He never did it again.

Dad and Mom, 1948

Chapter 10

⁓

CONTROVERSY

In 1944 Rev. Richard Veldman, the second pastor at First Protestant Reformed Church, had taken a call to the newly organized Fourth Protestant Reformed Church, later known as Southeast. The congregation of First had called Rev. Hubert De Wolf to take his place, and he had accepted the call. Now the consistory decided that the church should have a third man, because at this point it did not appear that Dad would be able to resume as much of his work as he had done before, and at any rate, there was enough work for a third man. From the nomination the congregation called Rev. Cornelius Hanko. This was very much against the wishes of Rev. De Wolf, and he sent a letter to Rev. Hanko saying, "No need for you to come, Case, we're doing just fine." At the same time Rev. Hanko received a letter from Dad that said, "Please come, Case; there's trouble." He came. It was 1948. No doubt it was the controversy over conditional theology that Dad meant when he spoke of trouble, for that had begun, also in First Church.

From the start we loved Rev. Hanko. He was endlessly patient with Dad. Dad needed that, for himself and others in his slow recovery, but so did the congregation. Rev. Hanko led our rather new Mr. and Mrs. Society. There was already tension there too; the question of conditions in God's covenant had inserted its ugly nose into our social get-togethers, and now into our societies. Rev. Hanko tended to have a calming influence, although it was hard on him. He never compromised.

Now we must backtrack a little and look at the circumstances in the United States at this time. World War II had broken out in 1941 when the Japanese attacked Pearl Harbor and had widened to include Germany, so that our troops were in both the East and the West. Much of our attention had been centered on the Netherlands, where many of our people had relatives and where our contact with the church was.

The war was not over when Dad received a strange letter in the mail. It was from a nephew of whom he was not aware, "Neef Case." Apparently the Dutch might correspond in the United States only with relatives. Therefore someone had adopted Dad to be his uncle in order to communicate with him. The writer told about the pressing needs of the people there, as well of the happenings in the church. He said that there had been a schism in the church that resulted in two factions, the liberated and the synodicals. Dr. Schilder was aligned with the liberated. But the liberated view of the covenant—that the covenant was conditioned on man's faith—was a belief that Dad had always opposed and had battled during his entire ministry. He had been confronted with it already in his seminary years. It had been taught by Prof. William Heyns. Dad was dumbfounded. "I can't believe it," he said as he paced the floor. "Dr. Schilder a Heynsian?"

Dad searched the Dutch papers and decided that his new

nephew was Dr. C. Veenhof. He acted on his conjecture and found that he had guessed correctly. He began to correspond with Dr. Veenhof. He found out that Dr. Schilder had been imprisoned by the Germans for a time but was released. Interestingly enough, one of the last papers Schilder had been allowed to read before he was put in prison was a copy of the *Standard Bearer*, in which Dad had written an editorial entitled, "Hitler, the Servant of the Lord." Obviously Dad did not mean those words the way the Nazis interpreted them.

Dad passed on to our people whatever he learned about the needs of their fellow Christians in the Netherlands, and they responded generously. As soon as they could, they began to send boxes there. One of the most pressing needs was for bicycle tires, for bicycles were the most common means of transportation in that low country. Box after box was shipped to the Netherlands. Our people took delight in giving and gave liberally.

In 1947 Dr. Schilder came to the United States for a second visit. It was late summer, and Dad was only partly recovered from the severe stroke he had suffered in June. They visited together and had a couple of backyard picnics, but no real discussions. Dad simply was not up to that. Then Dr. Schilder left to tour the United States.

In the fall he returned, and Dad was sufficiently recovered to attend a conference between Dr. Schilder and as many Protestant Reformed ministers as could attend. The subject was the covenant. It was obvious that Dad and Dr. Schilder differed broadly in their covenant views; yet they parted amicably, having simply agreed to disagree. Dr. Schilder held to a conditional covenant. Dad taught that the covenant was absolutely unconditional.

Here in the United States some of Protestant Reformed ministers in the West had made some independent decisions. The churches had been using uniform catechism books, approved by synod. Now the churches in the West decided to write their own material. Dad commented on this, saying that it was an inclination toward independentism. That comment was not well received.

I remembered the time when Dad lay sick in Sioux Falls, and one of the western ministers had visited and told him, "Don't worry; we'll take over now." Is that why these ideas were emerging? Were there some who were disappointed that he had recovered to the extent that he had, some who wanted to have a little more influence?

In First Protestant Reformed Church, where Dad, Rev. De Wolf, and Rev. Hanko were pastors, many discussions, sometimes heated, went on among the people. The question being discussed was whether or not you could speak of conditions in the covenant. Could you do that in a Reformed sense? Could you speak of conditions that God fulfills? Some friendships died; others suffered.

In the middle of this dissension, Rev. De Wolf preached a sermon on "The Rich Man and Lazarus," in which he said, "God promises to everyone of you that, if you believe, you shall be saved." To this day I do not know how he fit those words into that text.

The sermon brought protests, but he had his supporters. The congregation was in confusion. While the people were still talking about that sermon, Rev. De Wolf preached another. It was on conversion, from Matthew 18:3: "Except ye be converted, and become as little children, ye shall not enter into the kingdom of heaven." It was a beautiful text, but in the course of his sermon it was explained as something we had to do ourselves: "Our act of conversion is a prerequisite to enter into the kingdom."

Protests came from the congregation. It was in turmoil. Some thought that there was nothing wrong with those sermons. Others insisted that Rev. De Wolf should retract those words. The consistory said he had to apologize. He refused.

The matter went to classis. Classis reiterated the judgment of the consistory. It sent the classical committee to the consistory to deliver the decision personally. Rev. Vos was the spokesman and pleaded eloquently with Rev. De Wolf. He asked for time. The consistory gave him time. But De Wolf, instead of apologizing, told the congregation that he was sorry they had misunderstood him, not sorry for what he had said.

The next night the consistory, with the advice of a neighboring consistory, suspended him. Rev. De Wolf had said that he would recognize no suspension. Therefore, to avoid any confrontation on the Lord's day, the consistory obtained the use of the spacious auditorium of Grand Rapids Christian High School. There we met on that Sunday, and as it turned out, many Sundays thereafter.

On that first Sunday we had no idea how many would be faithful to the truth of the gospel, but as we pulled up to the school, we saw many cars parked there. When we opened the doors to the auditorium, we saw that it was nearly full. We knew that it did not matter how many were there, but it was natural that we were pleased that so many of our church family had joined us.

On that morning Dad preached on "Will ye also go away?" from John 6:67. It was an appropriate text for the occasion.

We met there for almost three years, while we sued to get the church property back. Midweek meetings, society meetings, and catechism classes, as well as the theological school, were held in the recently built Adams Christian School. God provided for us more than adequately. The hardest part, as I recall, was that family and friends were sometimes separated. We were no longer one in the faith.

That was true in our immediate family too. It was a source of grief to my parents. Herm did not want to belong to a church that would dispute over doctrine, so he went to a Reformed (RCA) church. Jo was married to Lambert Doezema, one of the ministers of the schismatics. Homer was minister in Doon, Iowa, which remained faithful. Bill and Jeanette belonged to Kalamazoo church; the majority of that church had gone with the De Wolf group. Nonetheless, a small group persisted until they could once again be constituted as a church, and Bill and Jeanette and other friends of ours remained with that group, often driving fifty miles to Grand Rapids to go to church with us, until they once again had a church of their own. But we became closer in the family of God.

When he knew there was going to be a court trial concerning ownership of the church property, Dad prepared scrupulously. When the case came to court, those who had left First Protestant Reformed Church had hired the same lawyer, Attorney Linsey, who had represented the Christian Reformed opposition in 1925. Linsey opened his remarks with an obvious attempt to put Dad at a disadvantage as he called him to the witness stand. "Well, *dominie*, here we are again, after about thirty years; is that right?" Dad: "That is evident." Linsey: "I wonder what another thirty years will bring." Dad's reply shook the lawyer: "I'll be in heaven, Mr. Linsey; where will you be?" The judge ordered that opening sally stricken from the record, but it had had its effect.

I think Mr. Linsey had forgotten too about the time that he and Dad had been on the same train. Linsey was playing cards; Dad was reading. Finally Linsey walked over to where Dad was sitting and said, "Why don't you play cards? Do you think it's a sin?" Dad replied, "I think it's because men like you play cards." Linsey had failed to bait Dad once, and now he failed again.

Dad had prepared well, planning not only what *he* should say, almost too thoroughly, but also visualizing what his opponents would say in return. As it turned out, the case hinged on which group was part of the corporation that was the Protestant Reformed Churches. And we were. Our lawyer represented us well. Ironically, we won that case on basically the same grounds that we had lost on in 1925; then we were not part of the corporation that was the Christian Reformed Church. (I could not help thinking about the time Rev. De Wolf had said from the pulpit, "Some of you carry the name 'Protestant Reformed' on your lapels like a badge of honor.")

The De Wolf group appealed to the Michigan Supreme Court. Their appeal was not sustained. In March 1956 the congregation of First Protestant Reformed Church could move back into its church after almost three years.

Chapter 11

~~~~~

LOOKING AHEAD

We had been decimated, not only in our congregation but in the entire denomination, for the schism had spread throughout all the Protestant Reformed churches. Those who had left us as a group returned to the Christian Reformed Church, confessing what they had once said was wrong doctrine, apparently without any twinges of conscience. Just what had they been disputing about? Bricks? Obviously being Protestant Reformed was not very important to them.

It was 1956, time to look ahead. The congregation needed fewer seats than the 1,300 in the auditorium of First Church. The seats were reconfigured, and the auditorium was refurbished. An excellent committee planned and oversaw the project. It was beautiful. The congregation worshiped there until the neighborhood changed and it was no longer safe to hold midweek meetings—catechism classes and societies—there. Then that property was sold and a new church was built in northeast Grand Rapids. I was always glad that Dad went to glory before he had to see all of these changes; not that they weren't necessary and good, but I think they would have been a little painful for him. However, perhaps, he would have rejoiced to see the next generation still optimistic and forward-looking.

Even with all of the remodeling going on, we could meet in our own church again. I do not remember what Dad's sermon topic was on the Sunday we were back in our own auditorium. I remember that it felt good—and a little strange. Our church life resumed its previous pattern of midweek meetings, catechism classes, and special events. Was it as if we had never been gone? No: many there were who had left and never came back, and we missed them.

I wonder if Dad sat down at that old pump organ when he came home from church on that first Sunday morning. He had not lost his ability to play it after his stroke. Nor had he lost his interest in the church world. He was always interested in what was happening on the church scene. He had more than one reason for this: I think he felt a responsibility toward his own people to make them alert to the many events going on out there, as long as we were in the church militant. More than that, in those days of ease of communication, God was giving us increased opportunities to sound the Reformed truth far and wide, and we had better do it. It was not Dad's church he was writing about: it was God's. And so he went on, surveying, analyzing, and commenting.

All the while he had built up a wealth of material from his many years of preaching and teaching, material that would be published in the future. He was meticulous in organizing what he wrote: he could lay his hand on it at any time. He did not keep it all in his study; that would have been hopeless. It lay on the attic floor. That was one reason the attic was off limits for us as children. Perhaps that was also the reason that there was no railing around those steps: Dad could simply walk partway up and lay his finished material along the edge.

After the schism the theological school was once again meeting in a classroom in the church basement. It was a humble place, but Dad never talked as if he felt he should have something better. He was content to teach "his boys." (He would probably have been amazed if he had had the opportunity to teach in the building that is the Protestant Reformed seminary building today, although I know of some men who had the dream of a seminary building long before it became a reality.)

I do not think Dad and Rev. Ophoff taught in the theological school on the same days, but they might have, because there was more than one classroom. Dad would dress as carefully as if he were going to teach a hundred. He would get up on time, put on a suit and a clean white shirt and a tie, and come downstairs for breakfast. Then he would walk through the back door and the garage and over to the side door of the church and make his way to the basement classroom. There he would spend the morning, except for a brief interlude when he would come home for coffee.

The afternoons were spent in various ways. Often he had writing to do: perhaps an article for the *Standard Bearer* or a speech he had to give; of course, he took his afternoon walk. He prepared carefully for his Wednesday evening catechism class too, a class that was started in Eastern Avenue and continued all of Dad's active years. That class studied the book of Revelation, among other subjects; the material later was the basis for the book *Behold, He Cometh!*

Sometimes, to relax, he would take up his oil paints; he usually painted in his study. Sometimes with a borrowed forge and anvil he had gotten from Louis Ebling, he would work in the blacksmith shop he had made in the basement. Mr. Ebling had a shop on

Wealthy Street. Dad had a workbench too, where he fashioned various pieces of furniture: a sewing cabinet for my mother, a chest of drawers for my sister, a dresser for me, stilts for my brother and me. He never lacked for something to do to relax, something creative.

In the summer you might find him in the garden. At first it was a flower garden. He grew roses to please my mother. We had a trellis at the entry to the garden; there were benches facing each other, and he planted climbing roses on each side, so that they grew over the top. But during World War II it became a victory garden; the government suggested that we raise vegetables, so that the nation's resources could be utilized by our fighting men. He grew green beans, yellow beans, pole beans—many varieties. We had a machine to cut up *sneebonen* (French-style beans). Dad attached a motor to it. At first Mom canned them all; later they bought a freezer and she froze them. The freezer was an upright and stood in the hall off the kitchen.

I don't think the soldiers got any more vegetables because Dad grew them. Neither did his diet become any more healthy, at least not until he had a severe stroke. His favorite lunch was some bacon with a piece of bread (or two) dipped in bacon grease and covered with syrup.

Dad in his garden

Even while he was growing vegetables, he had part of the garden reserved for flowers. For a while he grew dahlias, and every fall he had to dig up the bulbs and store them; but he always grew a few roses, because he knew they were Mom's favorite.

Saturday was spent with the family as long as we owned a car. If it was a warm summer day, we went to the beach and had a picnic. Dad did not go by the calendar when it came to swimming: one day in March, when the thermometer read eighty degrees, he said, "Let's go swimming." We went to Green Lake, less than twenty miles away. The ice had been out of the lake for three days. We ran in and ducked and ran out again, but Dad took a swim as if the water were seventy degrees.

After we were all married and out of the house, Dad still took Mom for a ride on Saturday afternoons. They did not take lunch along anymore; they went somewhere for supper, often to the Schnitzelbank, which was one of their favorite places. The waitresses knew him and gave the two of them a little extra attention.

As long as I can remember, Dad did not study on Saturdays. By that time his sermons were a "part of him." Sometimes he left the breakfast table early on Sunday morning, not, I think, to continue to prepare, but to keep his mind on his sermon

Green Lake, March 22, 1936

rather than be distracted by our talk. I do not know what he did when none of his children were home to distract him.

Both Dad and Mom made a practice of visiting the doctor for medical examinations once a year, and they both usually received a clean bill of health. Actually, I think Mom was stronger at that time than she had been in her childbearing years. But in about 1960 she came home from that exam with a slightly different report: the doctor had found a tumor on her thyroid gland, and although he did not believe it was likely to be malignant, nonetheless it should be removed.

The surgery was performed, and the tumor was not malignant, just as the doctor had expected. But Mom did not seem to get her strength back. Dad's care for her was touching. He would hardly let her do anything anymore. Etta was there a lot, of course, but Dad prepared some meals and took Mom out very often.

Then one morning the phone rang, and it was Dad. "Lois? Can you come over and fix Mom up a little? I don't know what's the matter with her, but she just sits there. Just do her hair, and make her look nice." And so I went.

I found things just as Dad had described them. Mom sat by the table in the breakfast room, a little smile on her face. I talked to her, but she did not answer me; she just smiled. I brushed her hair, but Etta had already gotten her dressed, and we decided to bring her to her favorite chair in the living room.

We had trouble getting her there, but she made it. I called the siblings I could reach. After supper Herm came over. When he saw her and tried to talk to her, he immediately said, "She's had a stroke." I could have kicked myself for my stupidity. I don't know whether anything could have been done for her, had I recognized the symptoms for what they were, but I had had no experience at all with stroke victims.

We made a bed for her downstairs, and I stayed with her. In the morning, even with my sister-in-law Trude's help, I could not get her on a commode. I told Dad I was going to call her doctor. He came in a little while and almost immediately suggested we take Mom to Pine Rest. It was known for being a psychiatric hospital, but it also had a fine geriatric department. Two of Mom's sisters had spent their last days there.

Dad was adamant. Mom was not going there. I think he felt he was losing her, and he was not going to let go. Finally we called Rev. Hanko. He came and talked quietly to Dad, and reluctantly Dad gave his consent. It was then the doctor spoke those grim words: "Just wait until your dad has to go there; and he will." An ambulance came and took Mom to Pine Rest.

Every day Dad went to visit her. Every day he tried to get her to talk to him, but she never did. Nor would she talk to anyone in the family. Yet the ladies in her Ladies Aid Society said that she talked with them every time they visited her.

She lived there for half a year, and then, on September 23, 1964, she passed away. Rev. Hanko preached her funeral sermon on Hebrews 13:8: "Jesus Christ the same yesterday, and to-day,

The last known pictures of Dad

and forever." Dad would have liked to preach it himself; he could hardly do that. But on Sunday morning Dad preached on John 11:25: "I am the resurrection and the life."

About this time Dad had to get his driver's license renewed, and he failed the vision test. He went to his oculist to get new glasses, but the doctor told him new glasses would not help, because his eyes were deteriorating. Dad wrote a letter to the Secretary of State. I never found out what was in that letter, but his license was renewed by return mail. I no longer dared to let our children ride with him, even though that had been one of his delights.

Now Dad began to get confused on the pulpit. He was still preaching, but Homer, now a professor in the seminary, was helping him with the communion services. Then one Sunday he became mixed up as he was announcing a song. I do not recall what song it was, but he stopped as he was reading the words and then said, "My eyes are all right; the words are mixed up." A titter of amusement went through the audience, of course.

Dad recovered himself, but his consistory realized it was time for him to quit preaching. That week a delegation from his consistory came to see him and reluctantly told him. I was there and do not remember who came, but they were kind and gentle, and he took it much better than I would have expected.

Then I had to spend two weeks in the hospital. When I came home, I was forbidden to leave the house for a while. The next day, in the morning, I had an urgent call from Trude. She had gotten a call from Etta, who apparently was at the end of her rope. She knew that I could not come, but she simply did not know what to do. Dad was being uncooperative, no matter what she asked of him. And he kept saying, "Just take me to Pine Rest."

I was at a loss: my sister in Kalamazoo was teaching school;

my brother, also in Kalamazoo, was working; another sister, as I recall, was in Canada; and brother Homer was teaching in the seminary.

I think that if I could have gone over there, I could have settled Dad down and perhaps postponed the time when he could no longer be home. And I could imagine that Dad was tired of having everyone tell him what to do. I was a daughter, not a daughter-in-law. He might have listened to me. But I could not go. And so I replied to Trude, "Maybe the time has come, then; it looks as if there's no other choice but to bring him to Pine Rest."

To Homer fell the task of bringing Dad to Pine Rest, after Homer had called that institution and made arrangements. As they were going out the back door, one of the women who sometimes brought meals and other goodies met them, and Dad said to her, "They're taking me to Pine Rest, Mrs. —."

After that, the telephones must have buzzed. The story was spread through all the congregation and to anyone who would listen. We had to restrict his visitors at the request of Pine Rest, because although they meant well, they were upsetting him. I thought of the ominous words his doctor had spoken when we had to bring Mom there: "Just wait until your dad has to go to Pine Rest; and he will."

I'm sure that he was not envisioning a situation like this when he spoke those words. Our people simply did not understand that Pine Rest was more than a hospital for the mentally ill. Even Dad, when talking about the time Mom had to be hospitalized at Pine Rest in the last days of her life, always said, "Ma went crazy." Our people thought we were mistreating him. The very idea that we would even think of mistreating him still makes me a little indignant, even after so many years.

That was not true of everyone. I well remember the kind lady who brought us a large pan of delicious chicken soup for supper. It was truly "comfort food."

Dad must have suffered more small strokes, because he soon lost his ability to walk. I was able to see him several times a week, and each time he went down a little farther. But whenever I saw him, he was well cared for.

Once I said to him, "Dad, do you still have that 'blessed hope' that you often talked about?" It was from Titus 2:13. He was almost indignant in his reply, as if to say, "How could you even ask?" He answered, "Of course I do!" in a ringing tone. I knew it: I just wanted to hear him say it. And he did, emphatically.

On September 2, 1965, God took him home to be with all the saints and angels, as Dad himself had often said, "To behold the glorious face of our Lord." Rev. Marinus Schipper preached his funeral sermon on Deuteronomy 33:27, "The eternal God is thy refuge, and underneath are the everlasting arms."

We will see him again, but no longer as "just Dad."

Dad wrote the following letters to his children when he took a trip to Europe in 1929. In order of age they were Johanna, Jeanette, Herman, Homer, and Lois. These letters are reproduced as they were handwritten. Because they are difficult to read in this form, for clarity they are also given in typewritten form. These letters are furnished courtesy of Ryan Doezema, my oldest nephew.

Dad's first two letters were written en route on the *Aquitania*, the ship that took him to Europe and the sister ship of the *Mauretania* and the *Lusitania*. The third letter was written from the Netherlands. The next three letters were written from Paris, and the last letter was again written from the Netherlands as he was preparing to come home.

First Protestant Reformed Church
FULLER AVENUE AND FRANKLIN STREET
GRAND RAPIDS, MICHIGAN

REV. H. HOEKSEMA
1139 FRANKLIN ST., S.E.
TEL. DIAL 23417

Aquitania July 8-29

Miss Johanna T. Hoeksema.

Dear daughter: —

Will just begin a little letter for you to-day and add a little to it every day. Then you will surely know that I thought about you daily. Ofcourse, you know that anyway. But here is the proof. You ought to see this boat! Boy—it's a monster! Will tell you more about it tomorrow, D. V. Good night, darling! Pray for father— and think about the calendar!

July 9-29

Hello, Johanna, here I am again and before I go to bed, I will add a little to this letter. Will just give you an idea how big the boat is. It is wider than Franklin St. and longer than from Fuller to Alto (That's the next street, is it not?) And from the bottom to the top deck it is higher than our Church-steeple. Good night, darling!

July 10-29

Another day past, Jo! I suppose you were rather surprised today, when you received that telegram. Isn't it wonderful, that I can be so far away and in the middle of the ocean and yet send a message to you as if I were somewhere in Iowa? It makes me feel that I am not so far away from you after all. It costs a little more than from Iowa — but you

114

Aquitania July 8–29

Miss Johanna D. Hoeksema

Dear daughter:

Will just begin a little letter for you today and add a little to it every day. Then you will surely know that I thought about you daily. Of course, you know that anyway. But here is the proof. You ought to see this boat! Boy—it's a monster! Will tell you more about it to-morrow, D.V. Good night, darling! Pray for father—and think about the calendar!

July 9–29

Hello, Johanna, here I am again and before I go to bed, I will add a little to this letter. Will first give you an idea how big the boat is. It is wider than Franklin St. and longer than from Fuller to Alto. (That's the next street, is it not?) And from the bottom to the top deck it is bigger than our church-steeple. Good night, darling!

July 10–29

Another day past, Jo! I suppose you were rather surprised today, when you received that tele-gram. Isn't it wonderful, that I can be so far away and in the middle of the ocean and yet send a mes-sage to you as if I were somewhere in Iowa? It makes me feel that I am not so far away from you after all. It costs a little more than from Iowa—but as you know — I don't worry about that. Well, good night darling! Feel good and don't forget me. And be a good girl. Good night! * * ...

July 11 - 29

Well, my girl, this time you are probably interested to know what I ate today. Yesterday I gave sister a report of my meals. And, surely, the sea-air makes me hungry and I can eat three times a day, allright. My steward woke me up this morning when he brought coffee in my room at 7:15. Then I read my bible a while and prayed. Thereupon I took a bath, that was all ready for me. Then - at 8:30 I had breakfast - grapefruit, grapenuts, bread, milk. At 11 oclock I had a cup of consommé with a cracker, at 1 oclock luncheon - soup - roast leg of lamb, baked-in-jacket potatoes & lettuce and tomatoes - bread and coffee and gooseberry-pie. Tonight: soup - roast loin of beef - boiled potatoes, carrots, coffee, bread and pastry. Pretty good he? Good night darling!

July 12 - 29

Just a few words today - tomorrow I must close this letter and then mail it. I can get stamps on the ship and mail it here too, and then the letter will leave as soon as possible. I wish you could see me sit here in my cabin — then I could see you too! And wouldn't I like that! Good night Jo!

July 13 - 29

Sunshine and cheer on desk today. I must close, now, my girl. Saw a few fishing boats already. Soon expect to see the first land. Good bye, sweetheart. Here is a big kiss *. Regard to Alta. With love,
your father.

116

know—I don't worry about that. Well, good night darling! Feel good and don't forget me. And be a good girl.
Good night! **

<u>July 11–29</u>

Well, my girl, this time you are probably interested to know what I ate today. Yesterday I gave sister[1]
a report of my meals. And, surely, the sea-air makes
me hungry and I can eat three times a day, allright.
My steward woke me up this morning when he brought
coffee in my room at 7:15. Then I read my Bible a while
and prayed. Thereupon I took a bath, that was all ready
for me. Then—at 8:30 I had breakfast—Grapefruit,
Grapenuts, bread, milk. At 11 oclock I had a cup of
consommé with a cracker, at 1 oclock luncheon—soup—
roast leg of lamb, baked-in-jacket potatoes—lettuce and
tomatoes—bread and coffee and gooseberry-pie. Tonight:
soup—roast loin of beef—boiled potatoes, carrots, coffee,
bread and pastry. Pretty good hé? Good night darling!

<u>July 12–29</u>

Just a few words today—tomorrow I must close
this letter and then mail it. I can get stamps on the ship
and mail it here too, and then the letter will leave as
soon as possible. I wish you could see me sit here in my
cabin—then I could see you too! And wouldn't I like that!
Good night Jo!

<u>July 13–29</u>

Sunshine and cheer on deck today. I must close,
now, my girl. Saw a few fishing boats already. Soon expect to see the first land. Good bye, sweetheart. Here is
a big kiss *. Regards to Etta. With love, your father.

[1] *Dad's name for Jeanette was often "Sister" or "Sis."*

First Protestant Reformed Church
FULLER AVENUE AND FRANKLIN STREET
GRAND RAPIDS, MICHIGAN

REV. H. HOEKSEMA
1139 FRANKLIN ST., S.E.
TEL. DIAL 23417

Aquitania - July 8-29

Miss Lois Eunice Hoeksema.

Dearie!

How are you, sweetheart? Have you been a good girlie, today? When you get this it will be almost your birthday. What a big girl you are already! Good night darling!

July 9 - 29.

Hello Loisie! Papa is far away from you now - but he is thinking about you and hopes soon to see you again! What were you doing today? Been playing all day, I suppose. Good night, sweetheart!

July 10 - 29.

And now I must write my little girlie a letter yet. You know darling I am writing a little every day, just to show you that I am not forgetting you at all. I suppose that you are almost getting ready for bed, while I am writing this to you. Well, write again tomorrow. Good night my girlie! x x x

July 11 - 29.

Another day is past again and I must

118

Aquitania July 8–29

Miss Lois Eunice Hoeksema

Dearie!

How are you, sweetheart? Have you been a good girlie, today? When you get this it will be almost your birthday. What a big girl you are already! Good night darling!

July 9–29

Hello Loisie![1]

Papa is far away from you now—but he is thinking about you and hopes soon to see you again! What were you doing today? Been playing all day, I suppose. Good night, sweatheart!

July 10–29

And now I must write my little girlie a letter yet. You know darling I am writing a little every day, just to show you that I am not forgetting you at all. I suppose that you are almost getting ready for bed, while I am writing this to you. Well, write again tomorrow. Good night my girlie! ***

July 11–29

Another day is past again and I must

---

[1] *Dad called me Loisie only in his letters, never in person.*

make this letter to my little Lois a little longer again. When I am writing this it's all dark already here, and the big sea looks so black! But I am not afraid of the sea, for Lord Jesus made the sea just as well as the land. And while it is late and all dark here, it is only afternoon with you and maybe you are playing in the sandbox yet. Well, be a nice girl darling and papa will soon come back to you. Good night, darling!

July 12-29

Again another day is past and before I go to bed, I must say good night to my little Lois yet. Let's see, what is your name again? Lois, Eunice..... Snip.... Hoeksema! Well, it won't be long, and I'll be back and be with you again. Do you pray for papa too, sweetheart? Good night, my girlie!

July 13-29

Well, my girlie, how are you this morning. I am feeling just fine. This is the last day that I can write from the boat. So now I must close this letter. Give my best regard to Etta. Good bye darling. Here's a big kiss for you! Bye, sweetheart. With love, Your father.

120

make this letter to my little Loisie a little longer again. When I am writing this it is all dark already here, and the big sea looks so black! But I am not afraid of the sea, for Lord Jesus made the sea just as well as the land. And while it is late and all dark here, it is only afternoon with you and maybe you are playing in the sandbox yet. Well, be a nice girl darling and papa will soon come back to you. Good night, darling!

July 12–29

Again another day is past and before I go to bed, I must say good night to my little Lois yet. Let's see, what's your name again? Lois, Eunice...Snip[1]... Hoeksema! Well, it won't be long, and I'll be back and be with you again. Do you pray for papa too, sweetheart? Good night, my girlie!

July 13–29

Well, my girlie, how are you this morning. I am feeling just fine. This is the last day that I can write from the boat. So now I must close this letter. Give my best regard to Etta. Good bye, darling. Here's a big kiss for you! Bye, sweetheart. With love, your father.

---

[1] *Dad sometimes called me "Snip" because he thought I was a bit sassy.*

First Protestant Reformed Church
FULLER AVENUE AND FRANKLIN STREET
GRAND RAPIDS, MICHIGAN

REV. H. HOEKSEMA
1139 FRANKLIN ST., S.E.
TEL. DIAL 23417

July 24 - 1929.

Dearest Johanna : —

Am writing this from Oldebark — a quaint and very neat little place. I thought of writing you a card again, but I must first try to get some. So I shall just write a few words to each of you, to let you know I am thinking of all of you and love you very much and very much long to see you all again. I was to my old home city today and looked it over. How very small things seem! Good night, darling! * * * —

From father.

Dearest Jeanette : —

How are you today? From your letter I am glad to notice that you still go swimming even though I am not home. Have you been to the lake already too? And have you been out otherwise already? To Athens, or to Kinneer's or with Vander Wal? Today I stood on many places I used to tread with wooden shoes on my feet. A queer feeling. Good night, sister dear. Here are some kisses. * * *. With love,

From father.

Dearest Herman : —

How are you? And have you other baby doves already? You wrote me that little blackie can fly too, and of that I am glad. But I am interested to know whether you have other little ones already. Remember I told you the story of how I needed a collar and found —

July 24–1929

Dearest Johanna:

Am writing this from Oldekerk—a quaint and very neat little place. I thought of writing you a card again, but I must first try to get some. So I will just write a few words to each of you, to let you know I am thinking of all of you and love you very much and very much long to see you all again. I was to my old home city today and looked it over. How very small things seem! Good night, darling! ***

From father.

Dearest Jeanette:

How are you today? From your letter I am glad to notice that you still go swimming even though I am not home. Have you been to the lake already too? And have you been out otherwise already? To Theule's, or to Timmer's or with Vander Wal's? Today I stood on many places I used to trod with wooden shoes on my feet. A queer feeling. Good night sister dearie! Here are some kisses. *** With love,

From father.

Dearest Herman:

How are you? And have you other baby doves[1] already? You wrote me that little blackie can fly too, and of that I am glad. But I am interested to know, whether you have other little ones already. Remember I told you the story of how I needed a collar and found

[1] *Herman and Homer raised pigeons.*

123

a dickie on the street? The spot where I found it, I saw today again. Good night my boy! * * *... From

Your father- with love,

Dearest Homer:-

I was very glad to receive a letter from you too. How nice now, that you can write now is'nt it? What a nice letter you wrote me! We have very nice weather here. Papa saw but very little rain and storm since he left home, and there is much need of rain here right now. Good night my boy! * * * with love,

from father.

Dearest Loisie:-

And what a nice letter you wrote me already! Was so glad to get it. I hope you are a nice girl and save up lot of kisses by the time I come back. Good night my little darling! Here are some kisses for you now. Bye, sweetheart.

With love,

father.

124

a dickie on the street? The spot where I found it, I saw today again. Good night my boy! *** From Your father—with love.

Dearest Homer:

I was very glad to receive a letter from you too. How nice now, that you can write now isn't it? What a nice letter you wrote me! We have very nice weather here. Papa saw but very little rain and storm since he left home, and there is much need of rain here right now. Good night my boy! *** With love,

from father.

Dearest Loisie:

And what a nice letter you wrote me already! Was so glad to get it. I hope you are a nice girl and save up lot of kisses by the time I come back. Good night my little darling! Here are some kisses for you now. Bye, sweetheart. With love, father.

Axour 12 - 1929

HÔTEL DU LOUVRE
PARIS

My very dearest children! —
As you notice by the paper
I am at present in Paris, the
big world - city, capital of
France, and centre of the
world's fashions.

I left Rotterdam this morning
at 10:28. Went through the
whole of Belgium and the
northern part of France. I passed
through a part of the battle -
ground of the world - war. Here
and there you could still see
the effects of the war. Especially
some ruins of old churches, that
used to be beautiful pieces of
architecture but were shot to
pieces during the war, were the
silent witnesses of the fierce conflict. We passed through St.

126

<u>August 12–1929</u>

My very dearest children:

As you notice by the paper I am at present in Paris, the big world-city, capital of France, and center of the world's fashion.

I left Rotterdam this morning at 10:28. Went through the whole of Belgium and the northern part of France. I passed through a part of the battle-ground of the world-war. Here and there you could still see the effect of the war. Especially some ruins of old churches, that used to be beautiful pieces of architecture but were shot to pieces during the war, were the silent witnesses of the fierce conflict. We passed through St.

Quentin where the battles raged especially during the early part of the awful war, and in that neighborhood we still saw many a ruin that reminded of the war.

But for the rest people here live as if they have already forgotten that awful period of the world's history. The ungodly do not learn righteousness, when the judgments of the Lord are in the earth.

Paris is a busy city. Yet, I do not think that it is quite as busy as London. I never was in a city, even in America, that is as busy as London. I believe, that in comparison with it, Paris is even quiet.

I am occupying a room on the 5 th floor again. I am sorry that there are no cards here with a picture

Quentin, where the battles raged especially during the early part of the awful war. And in that neighborhood we still saw many a ruin that reminded of the war.

But for the rest people here live as if they have already forgotten that awful period of the world's history. The ungodly do not learn righteousness, when the judgments of the Lord are in the earth.

Paris is a busy city. Yet, I do not think that it is quite as busy as London. I never was in a city, even in America, that is as busy as London. I believe, that in comparison with it, Paris is even quiet.

I am occupying a room on the 5th floor again. I am sorry that there are no cards here with a picture

of the hotel on them. For
I would like to send you
one of them and mark the
window of my room, so you
could see where I live for
the present.

Well, children, you know
a little about me again.

How are you all? Johanna,
are you enjoying a swim
once in a while? and you
too, sister? I suppose you
are helping mamma a good
deal and are trying to make
life pleasant and easy for
her. Then the little leaves
of the calendar will remain
clean, you know!

and Herman, how are you
getting along. I notice that
you have been working on
the farm again. Did you
like it? and did you do
any horseback-riding? Do

of the hotel on them. For I would like to send you one of them and mark the window of my room, so you could see where I live for the present.

Well, children, you know a little about me again.

How are you all? Johanna, are you enjoying a swim once in a while? And you too, sister? I suppose you are helping mamma a good deal and are trying to make life pleasant and easy for her? Then the little leaves of the calendar will remain clean, you know!

And Herman, how are you getting along. I notice that you have been working on the farm again. Did you like it? And did you do any horseback-riding? Do you learn to swim already?

And how is my Homer-boy? Enjoying your vacation are you? Do you ever go swimming too?

And Louise! You go to the pool in Franklin Park too, don't you? And Johanna wrote me that you weren't afraid at all. What a big girl you are getting to be already!

Well children, remember me, and don't forget to pray for me every day. I do for you all too. The time is getting shorter already. By the time you receive this letter it will almost be time for me to get on the boat again. And then we will count the days.

May the Lord bless you all and soon bring us together again! Goodbye, dearest children! Here's a big kiss for each of you *****. Your loving father you learn to swim already?

And how is my Homer-boy? Enjoying your vacation are you? Do you ever go swimming too?

And Loisie! You go to the pool in Franklin Park too, don't you? And Johanna wrote me that you weren't afraid at all. What a big girl you are getting to be already!

Well children, remember me, and don't forget to pray for me every day. I do for you all too. The time is getting shorter already. By the time you receive this letter it will almost be time for me to get on the boat again. And then we will count the days.

May the Lord bless you all and soon bring us together again! Good bye, dearest children! Here's a big kiss for each of you *****. Your loving father

First Protestant Reformed Church

FULLER AVENUE AND FRANKLIN STREET
GRAND RAPIDS, MICHIGAN

REV. H. HOEKSEMA
1139 FRANKLIN ST., S.E.
TEL. DIAL 32417

Paris.
Aug 15 - 1929.

Dear Jo :-

Just a little letter to you personally.
For, if I write all the letters to mama
and you all together, I am afraid I
will get a scolding.

Well, I am still in Paris. Tomorrow
I expect to leave again for Rotterdam
and then I know not how the program
will be. Perhaps I will go down to Elzas-
Lothar and come back down the Rhine.
I wrote to a certain pastor Neutsch in
Strassbourg, head of the institutions for
which we collected once. Remember that
lady in her nurse - clothes? Well, I asked
him if he could provide lodging for me
and show me the institutions and if he
answers that he can I will go for a few
days, the Lord willing.

Today I went seeing Paris again. I
went to two places especially, to a very
magnificent Catholic Church, a new one,
built after the war - and to the palace
at Versailles, outside of Paris.

But if you want to know, what I
saw there, you must exchange letters with

Paris

Aug 15–1929

Dear Jo:

Just a little letter to you personally. For, if I write all the letters to mama and you all together, I am afraid I will get a scolding.

Well, I am still in Paris. Tomorrow I expect to leave again for Rotterdam and then I know not how the program will be. Perhaps I will go down to Elzas Lothar[1] and come back down the Rhine. I wrote to a certain pastor (Deutsch) in Strasbourg, head of the institution for which we collected once. Remember that lady in her nurse-clothes? Well, I asked him if he could provide lodging for me and show me the institution and if he answers that he can I will go for a few days, the Lord willing.

Today I went seeing Paris again. I went to two places especially, to a very magnificent Catholic church, a new one, built after the war—and to the palace at Versailles, outside of Paris.

But if you want to know, what I saw there, you must exchange letters with

[1] *Alsace Lothar was a region of France.*

the other children.

Pain is a godless city, for it is full of pride, idolatry and superstition,

Well, good bye, my darling. Hope to see you soon again. We pray for eachother don't we?

Here's a big kiss. ✳

With love –

Your father.

the other children.

Paris is a godless city, for it is full of pride, idolatry, and superstition.

Well, good bye, my darling. Hope to see you soon again. We pray for each other don't we?

Here's a big kiss. *

With love

Your father.

First Protestant Reformed Church

FULLER AVENUE AND FRANKLIN STREET
GRAND RAPIDS, MICHIGAN

REV. H. HOEKSEMA
1139 FRANKLIN ST., S.E.
TEL. DIAL 23417

Paris, Aug 15-1929

Dear Sister:—

I wrote Johanna, that I would continue my news in this letter. So if you exchange with all the others, you will have a complete story of my days work.

This morning I first went to a Catholic church, a tremendous and beautiful building. Almost everything in Paris is tremendous and and beautiful, you know. This church dedicated in Oct. 1919, almost a year after the world-war. It was built from contributions made by the French people during the war, and considered a good work by which God might be induced to help the French and deliver them from all their miseries and also that He might deliver the pope from his captivity. This I read in an inscription in the church.

What do you think I did there this morning? Well, I attended mass! The church was full when I got there, so I stayed and watched the priest reading the mass, changing the bread and wine into the body and blood of Christ and putting the former on the tongue of the kneeling worshippers, while he drank the

138

Paris, Aug 15–1929

Dear Sister:

I wrote Johanna, that I would continue my news in this letter. So if you exchange with all the others, you will have a complete story of my days work.

This morning I first went to a Catholic church, a tremendous and beautiful building. Almost everything in Paris is tremendous and beautiful, you know. This church was dedicated in Oct. 1919, almost a year after the world-war. It was built from contributions made by the French people during the war, and considered a good work by which God might be induced to help the French and deliver them from all their miseries and also that he might deliver the pope from his captivity. This I read in an inscription in the church.

What do you think I did there this morning? Well, I attended mass! The church was full when I got there, so I stayed and watched the priest reading the mass, changing the bread and wine into the body and blood of Christ and putting the former on the tongue of the kneeling worshippers, while he drank the latter alone!

Surely, the man is the most terrible corruption of the Lord's supper one could possibly imagine.

Good bye, sweetheart! I must continue my story in another letter.

Here's a big kiss *.

With love.

Your father.

latter alone!

Surely, the mass is the most terrible corruption of the Lord's supper we could possibly imagine.

Good bye, sweetheart! I must continue my story in another letter.

Here's a big kiss *.

With love.

Your father.

First Protestant Reformed Church
FULLER AVENUE AND FRANKLIN STREET
GRAND RAPIDS, MICHIGAN

REV. H. HOEKSEMA
1139 FRANKLIN ST., S.E.
TEL. DIAL 23417

Zurolle –
Aug. 22 - 1929.

Dearest children: –
Jo, Sis, Hermie, Rory and Loisie!
I have just finished a letter for mama,
and did not at first intend to write
anymore letters, but I changed my mind
about it. I know that you like a letter
from your only father and it certainly
gives me a feeling as if I am talking a
little while with you all. and I certainly
would like to do that in reality. But
then, the time is not far off when I
shall see you all again, the Lord willing. And I am longing for it, too aren't
you? I feel that I could enjoy this
trip much more than I really do, if
you only were all here. Now I am always longing for you all and especially
when I am all alone in a strange place,
as I am tonight, I feel rather lonesome.
But, then, I'll soon see you all again if
all is well. When you receive this letter
you can easily count the days, for I
must be on the boat two weeks from
next Saturday. So, if it takes almost
two weeks for this letter to reach you,
it will be only a little more than a
week after that and I'll be home again.

Zwolle[1]

<u>Aug. 22–1929</u>

Dearest children:

Jo, Sis, Hermie, Porcy[2] and Loisie!

I have just finished a letter for mama, and did not at first intend to write anymore letters, but I changed my mind about it. I know that you like a letter from your only father and it certainly gives me a feeling as if I am talking a little while with you all. And I certainly would like to do that in reality. But then, the time is not far off when I shall see you all again, the Lord willing. And I am longing for it, too aren't you? I feel that I could enjoy this trip much more than I really do, if you only were all here. Now I am always longing for you all and especially when I am all alone in a strange place, as I am tonight, I feel rather lonesome. But, then, I'll soon see you all again if all is well. When you receive this letter, you can easily count the days, for I must be on the boat two weeks from next Saturday. So, if it takes almost two weeks for this letter to reach you, it will be only a little more than a week after that and I'll be home again.

[1] *Zwolle was the capital of the province of Overijsel, the Netherlands.*
[2] *Dad meant to write "Porky," not "Porcy." Although slim as he grew older, when he was young Homer was chubby.*

www.ingramcontent.com/pod-product-compliance
Lightning Source LLC
Chambersburg PA
CBHW061146040426
42445CB00013B/1585